PRAISE FOR *A MILE WIDE*

"Jesus used great stories to illustrate lasting truths about life, faith, and how His people could engage both in the world more fully. Brandon has done the same in his most recent book. This book doesn't just invite into deeper water so we'll know more about Jesus, but so we'll become more like Him."

—BOB GOFF, *New York Times* bestselling author of *Love Does*

"*A Mile Wide* is going to help so many! Brandon's biblical insight on things like gospel identity, discipleship, and justice make this a book not to be passed over."

—CHRISTINE CAINE, bestselling author, activist, evangelist, and cofounder of the A21 Campaign

"I like Brandon Hatmaker. I like the way he leads, the way he lives, and the way he writes. This book will help you deep dive your faith and you won't want to come back up."

—MARK BATTERSON, *New York Times* bestselling author of *The Circle Maker*, lead pastor of National Community Church

"I love it when a book really reflects the heart and mind of the author, and this one absolutely does. Brandon is an intelligent thinker, a godly man, and a passionate pastor who lives and breathes a deeper gospel. This book is both freeing and inspiring, an invitation to a more beautiful and grounded vision of Christian faith."

—SHAUNA NIEQUIST, bestselling author of *Bread and Wine* and *Savor*

"Brandon Hatmaker flips our smudged lens of stale religion to a crystalline view of the expansive, transformative Good News. *A Mile Wide* is a guidebook on walking the Jesus-way of love and community. This is a must-read for every neighbor."

—SHANNAN MARTIN, author of *Falling Free: Rescued from the Life I Always Wanted*

"With a relatable approach and style, *A Mile Wide* invites readers to not be just hearers but doers of the Word. A particularly beneficial book for small groups and churches called to rededicate themselves to Gospel mission, *A Mile Wide* is a welcome exhortation to the work of the Gospel here and now."

—PRESTON YANCEY, author of *Out of the House of Bread: Satisfying Your Hunger for God with the Spiritual Disciplines*

"I love this book because I love Brandon Hatmaker and everything he does. But second, I love this book because Brandon articulates a robust spirituality derived with a larger view of the Gospel and one equal to the significant challenge of mission in our day."

—ALAN HIRSCH, founder of Forge, 100Movements, and Future Travelers; award-winning author, www.alanhirsch.org

"Countless times while reading *A Mile Wide*, I thought, *I want some of what Brandon has*. And that's because there's something unique about his Christian story—it's joy-filled, earnest, and believable, a kind that will pour life into your own."

—MATTHEW PAUL TURNER, bestselling author of *Churched* and *Our Great Big American God*

"Brandon Hatmaker offers up a God-inspired image of faith that proves practical, inspiring, and motivational . . . who knew engaging our faith at a deeper level could be this much fun?"

—STEVE HAAS, vice president and Chief Catalyst at World Vision US

"*A Mile Wide* will help readers unlock the need to go deeper in their pursuit of justice, love, grace, and truth. I've seen Brandon live out this book in the real world, and I know his desire is to see others do the exact same thing."

—CHRIS MARLOW, founder and CEO of Help One Now and author of *Doing Good Is Simple*

"In my world I have the great privilege of serving some incredible pastors and leaders, many of whom are great authors. Reading *A Mile Wide* reminded me that my friend Brandon is a world-class pastor, leader, and author. This book has the kind of depth my own heart was yearning for and the practical wisdom I can be using today to connect deeply with the heart of my loving Father."

—BRIAN CARPENTER, founder of Refuge Foundation

"What Brandon has here is a book that needs to be read over and over again. His words will make you look in the mirror and question everything you think you know about the Christian life. His anthem to trade shallow religion for a deeper faith is something all of us need to get behind."

—JARRID WILSON, author of *Jesus Swagger* and *Love Is Oxygen*

"*A Mile Wide* doesn't shy away from hard topics that every Christian should be considering . . . Within the first fifty pages, I had highlighted and marked sentences that challenged and convicted me . . . I found myself smiling because I could hear his voice in the call to a different and more true experience of Christ, but I smiled even bigger when I heard the voice of God doing the same through his words."

—ANGIE SMITH, Bible teacher and bestselling author of *Chasing God* and *Seamless*

"No matter who you are, *A Mile Wide* has something for you. Brandon approaches a deeper faith with such tenderness, you will not spend any time feeling guilty or proud over your faith journey. You will simply feel as though you are reading words from your big brother who cares for your soul and talks about how the good news of Jesus saves us, transforms us, and continues to interrupt our lives to help us see Jesus exactly where we are."

—JAMIE IVEY, host of the *Happy Hour* podcast

"I love *A Mile Wide*. Brandon Hatmaker reveals a bigger gospel and invites us into a greater kingdom. This book drips with dignity for humanity and a heart for God."

—LEROY BARBER, executive director of The
Voices Project and director of Hopemob

A
MILE
WIDE

A MILE WIDE

TRADING A SHALLOW RELIGION

FOR A DEEPER FAITH

BRANDON HATMAKER

NELSON
BOOKS

An Imprint of Thomas Nelson

Published in Nashville, Tennessee, by Nelson Books, an imprint of Thomas Nelson. Nelson Books and Thomas Nelson are registered trademarks of HarperCollins Christian Publishing, Inc.

The author is represented by Alive Literary Agency, 7680 Goddard Street, Suite 200, Colorado Springs, Colorado 80920, www.aliveliterary.com.

Thomas Nelson titles may be purchased in bulk for educational, business, fundraising, or sales promotional use. For information, please e-mail SpecialMarkets@ ThomasNelson.com.

Unless otherwise indicated, Scripture quotations are taken from the Holy Bible, New International Version®, NIV®. Copyright © 1973, 1978, 1984, 2011 by Biblica, Inc.™ Used by permission of Zondervan. All rights reserved worldwide. www.zondervan. com. The "NIV"and "New International Version" are trademarks registered in the United States Patent and Trademark Office by Biblica, Inc.™

Scripture quotations marked NLT are taken from the *Holy Bible*, New Living Translation. © 1996, 2004, 2007, 2013 by Tyndale House Foundation. Used by permission of Tyndale House Publishers, Inc., Carol Stream, Illinois 60188. All rights reserved.

Scripture quotations marked KJV are from the King James Version, public domain.

Scripture quotations marked NKJV the New King James Version®. © 1982 by Thomas Nelson. Used by permission. All rights reserved.

978-0-7180-8431-8 (IE)
978-0-7180-9293-1 (signed)

Library of Congress Cataloging-in-Publication Data

Names: Hatmaker, Brandon, 1972- author.
Title: A mile wide : trading a shallow religion for a deeper faith / Brandon Hatmaker.
Description: Nashville : Thomas Nelson, 2016. | Includes bibliographical references.
Identifiers: LCCN 2016004538 | ISBN 9780718078508
Subjects: LCSH: Christian life.
Classification: LCC BV4501.3 .H378 2016 | DDC 248.4--dc23 LC record available at https://lccn.loc.gov/2016004538

Printed in the United States of America

16 17 18 19 20 RRD 6 5 4 3 2 1

To Gavin, Sydney, Caleb, Ben, and Remy: I love you with everything I am. My prayer is that somehow through an imperfect earthly father you will increasingly find comfort in the grace and goodness of a perfect heavenly Father. May you each live life to the fullest.

To Jen: You keep me rooted. You inspire me. You challenge me to dig and then dig even more. You strengthen me. I love you.

To Jesus: Your grace is amazing. I'm no longer surprised, just amazed.

To those of you searching for more: Keep digging. Your treasure awaits.

CONTENTS

INTRODUCTION

IN 1889, AMERICAN journalist and humorist Edgar Nye introduced the phrase "A mile wide and an inch deep." He was referring to a river found in the midwestern and western United States, called the Platte River. The Platte is a muddy, wide, shallow, meandering stream with a swampy bottom. These characteristics made it too difficult to ever be used as a major navigation route. Though the Platte is an important tributary system in the Missouri River watershed, it was disqualified from use because of its lack of depth.

Nye wrote that the river "has a very large circulation, but very little influence. It covers a good deal of ground, but is not deep. In some places it is a mile wide and three-quarters of an inch deep."[1]

And so the phrase was born. It's not meant to be a compliment. In fact, it quickly began to be used in politics, academia, and other fields to describe people whose knowledge is superficial.

Recently the phrase has been used to describe the modern church and, even more indicting, those who call themselves believers. As someone who has spent more than twenty years in local church leadership, this kills me. Critics claim that as our churches continue to grow in size, they lack in depth. Though our programs and events are becoming more and more broad, they only skim the surface of truth. Worse, critics contend, most believers don't actually live what they say they believe.

As much as I don't want to admit it, there are elements of these accusations that ring true. From the beginning, believers have struggled between shallow religion and deeper faith. In a twist of irony (or accidental hypocrisy), it can be just as common for us to slip into religious legalism as it is to live like Jesus actually lived.

But it's one thing to have someone accuse you of a shallow faith. It's another to actually feel a lack of depth in your own life.

I've felt it. We probably all have. We go through weeks, months, and even years of hoping for more. We seek deeper relationships, bigger life changes, a more significant purpose, and more intimacy with God. We hope for a more transformed life that we know is possible. We crave more depth but can't seem to find it.

Maybe you're the opposite. It's quite possible that you're doing, feeling, and living better than you ever have. Some of you are on a spiritual high. Yet there's still a desire to dig deeper into the goodness you've found. No matter how deep you get, you find yourself hungry for more.

This is a good thing.

Jesus discussed a different kind of depth, not of water, but of soil. It's the kind of depth that results in more. In the parable of the four soils (parable of the sower) he taught how the quality and depth of the soil represents our heart's receptivity to his truth. Our receptivity determines the fruit, not the other way around. Instead of focusing on more fruit, we're challenged to focus on the condition of the soil.

In *A Mile Wide* we'll build on Jesus' idea of depth by first evaluating and expanding our view of the gospel. From there we'll explore how a bigger gospel tills the soil of our hearts as it continues to work in us and eventually through us. The fruit will be the exchange of a superficial or powerless religion for an ever-deepening and fulfilling faith. That depth you're craving is actually within reach.

Whether you are a lifetime believer, new to faith, or a skeptic of Christianity, my hope is that this book will change forever the way you view Christ, yourself, and others. With that in mind, my heart echoes for you Paul's prayer to the Ephesians:

> For this reason I kneel before the Father . . . I pray that out of his glorious riches he may strengthen you with power through his Spirit in your inner being, so that Christ may dwell in your hearts through faith. And I pray that you, being rooted and established in love, may have power, together with all the Lord's holy people, to grasp how wide and long and high and deep is the love of Christ, and to know this love that surpasses knowledge—that you may be filled to the measure of all the fullness of God. (Ephesians 3:14–19)

CHAPTER 1

A FULLER FAITH

"I have come that they may have
life, and have it to the full."

—JOHN 10:10

THE TENSION WAS palpable. A woman lay facedown in the shadows of the temple while her accusers stood by. As Jesus knelt in front of her, onlookers waited silently, as if frozen in time. With bated breath they anticipated his next words.

Exposed and shamed, she lay there accused . . . and guilty. Everyone knew this was a serious moment. She was a woman caught in adultery, literally in the act, a crime punishable by death. Her fate was not a humane or honorable death. Anyone caught in adultery was to be given the death of a heathen: public stoning by the spiritually deserving.

"In the law Moses commanded us to stone such women," they barked at Jesus.

The bait was set.

"What do you say, [*Rabbi*]?" (John 8:5).

Hell-bent on publicly condemning the guilty woman, the accusers were blinded by their agenda. They could not see the double standard and hypocrisy at play. She was merely a pawn. A life discarded in a web of deceit designed by the spiritually corrupt to trap Jesus.

His eyes locked onto hers. For a moment the mob seemed to fade into the periphery. It was as if only Jesus and the woman remained. Humiliated, she struggled to raise her chin to look back at him. The moment their eyes met . . . she knew she was no longer alone. Jesus would not abandon her. He would be her advocate.

The dust stirred as he began to write in the sand. The soil was as dry as her accusers' hearts, parched and in need of living water. History doesn't record what he wrote. Maybe the wind covered his words just as quickly as his finger carved out the letters.

Some believe he was listing the many sins of the accusers. I'm not convinced it matters what he wrote with his hands; with his eyes Jesus wrote mercy upon her heart, a new covenant marked by grace.

"Let any one of you who is without sin be the first to throw a stone at her," Jesus said without looking up (John 8:7).

All he had taught, all he lived for, and all he would die for was summed up in one statement. None of us are without guilt. "There is no one righteous, not even one" (Romans 3:10).

Like the light in an opening scene when it first illuminates what's behind the curtain, Jesus' words instantly exposed the hearts of the elders. Others pursed their lips as they internally justified their actions. But as truth seized the moment, one by one they began to release their grip on the stones and walk away.

Something incredibly beautiful happened in that moment. Everyone was put in their proper place. Jesus spoke the language of everyone within earshot. As an advocate he brought both conviction and confidence.

Over and over during the course of his life, Jesus identified himself physically with our humanity and our sin. Whether on his knees or on the cross, in so many ways he lowered himself to our level. His redemption offered dignity to the lowest of the low. And with his words he spoke grace into existence:

> "Woman, where are they? Has no one condemned you?"
>
> "No one, sir," she said.
>
> "Then neither do I condemn you," Jesus declared. (John 8:10–11)

She was legally guilty, yet Jesus declared her innocent.

This story reveals a crossroads for every believer. Both the religious leaders and Jesus claimed allegiance to the same God of Israel. Yet the religious held a different perspective regarding the law, how they viewed themselves, and how they viewed others.

They dug deep to accuse but skimmed the surface when looking at themselves. They applied the law to advance their agenda, minimized self-sacrifice, and prioritized anything that increased their authority, position, or wealth. Their law was to the letter. Their innocence was shallow. And their view of others lacked empathy.

> For what the law was powerless to do because it was weakened by the flesh, God did by sending his own son in the likeness of sinful flesh to be a sin offering. And so he condemned sin in the flesh, in order that the righteous requirement of the law might be fully met in us, who do not live according to the flesh but according to the Spirit. (Romans 8:3–4)

For Jesus, the law was just the beginning. He revealed a new kind of grace and goodness. He felt the deepest empathy, showed the greatest compassion, and offered the fullest hope. He put himself last, and he consistently made much of others. He taught us to peel back the layers of everything to see what's beneath.

He didn't just love us; he loved us with a godly love. He didn't just lower himself to the depths of mankind by becoming man himself; he considered equality with God something not to be grasped and instead made himself the son of man. Jesus lived incredibly deep. And he invites us to join him in the depths.

So let's get digging.

A DANGEROUS REALITY

It's easy to forget that the accusers from Scripture were the religious elite. They weren't your prototypical bad guys out to overcome good with evil. They were the hyper-spiritual leaders on a mission to protect their God and their religion. And they would go through, over, and around anyone to do it. They thought they were doing good, but the letter of the law had become their god.

This is a dangerous reality. We are at risk of doing the same, and unbeknownst to us, we often do. Our sin nature would have us choose sides, check lists, and oversimplify truth nearly every time. When we do so, we become like the accusers.

We are easily blinded when we slip into this shallow way of religion. It comes hand in hand with clouded vision and disillusionment. On paper we're doing what is right, so we can check the box and move on without conviction. We clearly see everyone else's shortcomings. We ourselves are legally without fault, so why would we have to consider how our actions affect or neglect others? Why worry about the abstract implications or collateral damage of our actions, posture, or words when what we've done or said was not technically wrong?

I guess the main reason is because that's exactly what Jesus spent the majority of his life teaching us to do: to love our neighbors. We are to consider deeply how the application of what we believe impacts how others view him and his kingdom. It's an exchange in how we think about everything.

Paul championed this same message and warned us against a shallow view of faith in his first letter to Timothy. He reminded Timothy that when we neglect love, we become like the teachers of the law, and that our interpretive lens should always be love. It's like the legend on a map helping us set our course. How then should we live? Choose love. Every time.

———

"The goal of this command is love," wrote Paul, "which comes from a pure heart and a good conscience and a sincere faith. Some have departed from these and have turned to meaningless talk. They want to be teachers of the law, but they do not know what they are talking about or what they so confidently affirm. We know that the law is good if one uses it properly" (1 Timothy 1:5–8).

Jesus couldn't have been clearer. He spoke directly to this when quizzed by the teachers of the law (Matthew 22:36–40). What is the greatest commandment? they asked. To love God and love others, Jesus replied. All the Law and the Prophets hang on these two.

Jesus came to rip the scales off our religious eyes to show us the heart behind the letters. He moved from judgment to grace and chose love over law and people over position. His gospel was for all, his community was inclusive, his discipleship was holistic, his mission was eternal, and his kingdom was vast. Everything about Jesus and his dream for us was bigger, wider, and deeper than we can imagine.

And in order to live a fuller faith, we must go on one of the greatest journeys of a believer's life: a journey down. As the rest of the world challenges us to keep climbing the ladder, Jesus repeatedly challenges us to descend. In an ironic twist, it's there in the depths that we find full life. But it doesn't come naturally. We have to check every motive, evaluate every decision, and be intentional with every pursuit. It's a constant discipline we have to learn to apply, and it starts with recognizing and understanding our need for depth.

RECOGNIZING OUR NEED FOR DEPTH

My dog has a fear of missing out (FOMO). And to be honest with you, it can be fairly entertaining. I think it has to do with the fact that she doesn't know she's a dog. She thinks she's one of the kids. In my family we've shortened the description of this reality to the initials F.O.M.O., pronounced just like it reads: "Fo-Mo." Makes for a great Twitter hashtag: #FOMO.

You can clearly see it when the house starts to bustle each morning. Everyone starts loading backpacks for school and eating breakfast . . . and there is Ladybird, underfoot. Staring puppy-dog eyes, ears laid back, and scared to death we're leaving for vacation instead of for the day. She's afraid she'll be left behind.

It's the same when the boys and their friends run down the stairs and quickly out the back door. Lady can come out of a dead sleep in the living room and magically transport herself to the window facing the yard. There they are, boys outside doing their thing, and Ladybird staring through the glass, tail wagging, waiting, vicariously living through their adventure. Wishing she was with them.

I think some of us have spiritual FOMO.

Most believers I know would say they thirst for more. "I want to go deeper," "I need to be fed," and "There's got to be more" are commonly heard inside and outside of the local church.

Spiritual FOMO is intrinsically a good thing. We are wired to crave more of God. So when we feel as if something is missing, it triggers a response that says, "Hey, whatever it is that I'm experiencing . . . it's not enough. There's something else."

And there usually is.

Our desire for "more" can come from either a healthy or an unhealthy place. Some of us have a healthy desire to know God more. We've "tasted and seen," and it's changed everything (Psalm 34:8). We've experienced firsthand the fullness of Christ and want more. But some of us are suffering the pangs of spiritual malnutrition. We want more because we need more. We're scraping by each day hearing about the feast but rarely dining at the table.

> **We're scraping by each day hearing about the feast but rarely dining at the table.**

The reason for our craving typically determines our response. Ironically, the bigger the void, the more desperately we search and the more likely we are to find substance. There's an emptiness we must experience in order to strip ourselves of all earthly recovery. It's a place where the only option is whatever God provides. It's a pure place. A necessary place.

On the flip side, for those of us who've encountered Jesus deeply, when we're hungry for more, we tend to return to the same table we've already experienced. We add another Bible study, join a new small group, start a new accountability group, or attend another worship service. We're doing more of the same things, expecting different results. Like a hamster on a wheel, we're working harder but not going any farther. We're hoping to create new depth, but instead we end up spreading ourselves thin. And there we are: *a mile wide and an inch deep.*

To avoid this phenomenon and actually move forward, let's discuss three key areas in which we are designed for more depth. While we'll dig into each in the coming chapters, let's first take a moment to name them so we can see where we personally might most need to dig in.

1. **Depth in understanding.** This is the most obvious area and is simply the desire to go deeper into God's Word. It is so very necessary. Simply put, we need to know what the Bible says. But we have to pursue truth with the right intentions. The teachers of the law loved knowledge for knowledge's sake and frequently missed the point and certainly missed the person of Jesus. Knowledge became their pursuit, and it resulted in pride. Learning but not living leads to a shallow life every time.

2. **Depth in relationships.** We each need a place where we can confess our deepest struggles and be received with an equally deep empathy and desire for healing. Unfortunately, we have a problem in the church with vulnerability, which is closely tied to the fear of judgment. Thus, many of us remain guarded and struggle to crack the nut on true community.

3. **Depth in spirit.** The Spirit urges us, leads us, and comforts us in different ways. At times the Spirit may move boldly and quickly, and at others he may whisper only when we are still and quiet. It's possible to be committed to Bible study, live in biblical community, yet be completely void of any spiritual vitality or depth. Maybe you're running the race but feeling spiritually malnourished.

It's important to take a look at our lives and see how we're doing in each of these areas. If we're honest, it probably won't take too much effort to find our weak spots. Are we biblically shallow, neglecting to learn the Scriptures or, worse, to apply the Scriptures we've learned? Are we relationally shallow, engaging in superficial relationships yet hungering for more vulnerability? Or are we spiritually shallow, going through all the motions of Christianity but neglecting the leadership of the Holy Spirit?

None of these is more dangerous than the other. Each can result in a feeling of or *fear of missing out*. But not one of them puts us beyond recovery.

UNDERSTANDING OUR NEED FOR DEPTH

For the majority of my life, whenever I felt that I was missing out (#FOMO), needed a word from God, or simply was not feeling as close to Christ as I needed to be, I would instantly assume I needed to do more. My natural response was to grow by adding something to my schedule. I hoped that by making myself busier doing church things, I would intuitively experience more Christian depth. But I didn't. I was just busier and had less time to slow down, be still, think, or listen. I did more but gave less to each endeavor. I became a *jack-of-all-trades*, but master of none.

A quick look at our calendars might give us an indicator as to whether we're spiritually thriving or just getting by.

Width does not create depth. If anything, it's the opposite. In many ways it's depth that determines our capacity for width. Jesus taught this concept in the parable of the four soils (parable of the sower), a beautiful illustration of how the receptivity and condition of our hearts determines the fullness of our faith. Each condition assumes a certain level of depth and a certain quality of depth.

> That same day Jesus went out of the house and sat by the lake. Such large crowds gathered around him that he got into a boat and sat in it, while all the people stood on the shore. Then he told them many things in parables, saying: "A farmer went out to sow his seed. As he was scattering the seed, some fell along the path, and the birds came and ate it up. Some fell on rocky places, where it did not have much soil. It sprang up quickly, because the soil was shallow. But when the sun came up, the plants were scorched, and they withered because they had no root. Other seed fell among thorns, which grew up and choked the plants. Still other seed fell on good soil, where it produced a crop—a hundred, sixty or thirty times what was sown. Whoever has ears, let them hear."
>
> The disciples came to him and asked, "Why do you speak to the people in parables?"
>
> He replied, "Because the knowledge of the secrets of the kingdom of heaven has been given to you, but not to them." (Matthew 13:1–11)

It's important to frame this parable well. It's meant to be a diagnosis, not a prognosis, and the central point is found in verse 9: "Whoever has ears, let them hear."

This is meant to be a temperature check, and we are all in need of spiritual examination. Humans are famously un-self-aware. We can see other people's flaws so much more clearly than we see our own. Yet, we are all soil in this story, not soil inspectors. We're not capable of that, because a lot of soil looks the same on the surface. The only person, besides Jesus, who can dig honestly beneath the surface of our hearts is us.

And here's the good news. Our diagnosis is not permanent, or inevitable. In fact, we are rarely just one type of soil all the time. I have been all four and at times have two coexisting soil types. I have receptive depth in one area but am shallow and hardened in another.

We manage a weird paradox where we can be both un-self-aware and also incredibly self-condemning. This parable should lead us to neither denial nor condemnation. Regardless of our circumstances, even the worst soil can be brought back to life.

We've all got ears, so the central question to ask of ourselves is: What kind of listener am I? Essentially we're asking, *How deep is my receptivity?* How do I typically receive God's Word, his instruction, his leadership, his ways? And what's getting in the way?

Before we look at the soils themselves, it's interesting to take a look at the disciples' response to this story. They wanted people to understand who Jesus was, yet Jesus was making it hard on them. Their desire to make things easy was getting in the way of them understanding the depth of his teaching.

"Why do you speak to people in parables?" they asked.

They didn't ask, "Why do you speak to *us* in parables?" They were already privy to the ways of Christ, but they were worried about the people.

In essence they were asking Jesus to make it simple. But Jesus knew something they didn't. His kingdom would come at an incredible cost. Presenting it as a low-hanging fruit might net way more early adopters who liked the advantages, but that kingdom would lack depth. And the early church had to be supernaturally strong to endure the next century without caving.

The true gospel has never appealed to the masses, *nor did it ever try to.* Jesus didn't want fans; he wanted followers. Yes, this kingdom will save your whole life, but you have to lose the one you have first. There is no resurrection without a death.

There is a danger in attempting to widen the front door that Jesus said would always be narrow. It is not narrow because God wants to keep people out. It is narrow because so few are actually willing to do what it takes to enter. Jesus taught the kingdom in a way that made sincere converts work for it. He drew them with depth and mystery and truth.

Here we see a mysterious partnership between God's sovereign preparation of our hearts—making us able to hear and understand—and our personal responsibility to be good hearers, to address the soil of our hearts.

In Matthew 13:14–15, quoting Isaiah 6:9–10, Jesus explained a willful blindness and deafness and hardness of heart that would never be receptive to salvation and transformation.

> "You will be ever hearing but never understanding;
> you will be ever seeing but never perceiving.
> For this people's heart has become calloused;
> they hardly hear with their ears,
> and they have closed their eyes.
> Otherwise they might see with their eyes,
> hear with their ears,
> understand with their hearts
> and turn, and I would heal them."

What kind of hearers are we? If we shut out the truth long enough, we may lose the ability to even notice it anymore. In Exodus, it says that after seeing all God was doing, Pharoah "hardened his heart" (8:15, 32; 9:34). Seeing, hearing, and understanding are necessary for depth, and we must be careful not to block those senses out.

Nothing matters more than humility, teachability, and repentance, because the opposites—pride, arrogance, and obstinacy—make us blind and deaf to every goodness and truth in the kingdom. We must not lose the power of our spiritual senses if we are to find the fullness that comes from spiritual depth.

Now, let's look more closely at the parable. There are three elements to consider in this story: the seeds, the sower, and the soil. The seeds represent the gospel, which brings forth fruit in souls. Jesus called it the "secrets of the kingdom" (Matthew 13:11), and it is packed full of life. The sower is Jesus, who teaches these life-packed words everywhere and anywhere there are people with ears. But the reception depends upon the receiver, the soil.

There are four kinds of soil mentioned in this story. It says that seeds fell on the path, on rocky ground, among the thorns, and on good soil. Each represents a condition of the heart and is an indicator of receptive ability.

The seed on the path never got past the top layer of soil. Never sank in. Not one inch. So many of us can recall the tilling season before Christ took root in our hearts, the tenderizing of our souls, searching, listening, asking questions . . . This soil is the opposite.

Verse 19 goes on to say, "When anyone hears the message about the kingdom and does not understand it, the evil one comes and snatches away what was sown in their heart. This is the seed sown along the path."

The gospel goes in one ear and out the other. It makes no impression and leaves no trace. The Greek word for "understand" in this verse means "consider"; thus there was no consideration, no delight in spiritual things, no fascination with God, no hunger for any of this truth. Hardened at the surface level and stuck there. Superficial. Shallow.

Characteristics that result in inhospitable soil to God's movement are cynicism, bitterness, entitlement, and arrogance. All are characteristics of the religious leaders of Jesus' day and a threat to us today. Jesus reminds us that we have a real enemy, and this is his favorite type of hearer.

Matthew Henry wrote, "Such mindless, careless, trifling hearers are an easy prey to Satan; who, as he is the great murderer of souls, so he is the great thief of sermons, and will be sure to rob us of the word, if we take not care to keep it: as the birds pick up the seed that falls on the ground that is neither ploughed before nor harrowed after."[1]

This person hears the Word, but it makes no sense. He finds no tenderness in any of it. The empty-hearted person says *no* to God.

The seed on rocky ground found itself on soil that was softer, but only at the surface. When people's hearts have this kind of soil, they are quick to hear, ready to receive, and the gospel bursts quickly right out. Scripture says they receive it "with joy" (v. 20).

This reminds me of my days as a youth pastor. Each year we would come back from summer camp, and the youth would lead the Sunday evening worship service. It was a "report from camp"–type event where students would lead worship and share a short testimony from their week.

One Sunday we had a middle school girl share how she'd had spiritual experiences before, but this time, *this* time, it was different. She assured us all that this was a mountaintop experience, and she was *never* coming down. *Never!*

We were all hopeful for her. We were encouraged by her zeal. But the adults in the room all knew from experience that life comes with both highs and lows—both are important to spiritual growth. And it was unrealistic to think that all of life would be peachy keen from then on.

Being moved by a week of good sermons is not the same as being transformed by the gospel. Transformation is the continuing work of the gospel in our lives that never stops. It's a lifelong journey, and we learn from this life. But take caution; the heart may melt under the Word but not be melted down by the Word.

Translated: the seed may have broken through, but without the process of purging the soil over time with the gospel of life, the roots have no place to grow. What was above ground outpaced what was below. The good soil was shallow.

> **Being moved by a week of good sermons is not the same as being transformed by the gospel.**

Without depth, the dazzle won't hold. We have to spend far more time nurturing what no one ever sees under the surface than worrying about what's above the soil. Things like Scripture and prayer and community root us so deeply. They are the unglamorous, unfancy work of discipleship. They fix our principles and resolutions; they root our habits and affections—they make us strong. They prepare us for what's to come. The same sun that warms and develops the well-rooted believer withers and burns up those who aren't.

The seed among thorns is at first received deeply. Scripture tells us that it was well-rooted and bearing fruit. But there is a necessary practice for a fruit-bearing plant to stay healthy: weeding.

That the thorns "grew up" (v. 7) suggests they weren't there when the seed was sown but attacked later, once the seed was already developing. Where, in the last soil, rocks spoiled the root, here the thorns spoiled the entire plant.

Jesus explains this soil in verse 22: "The seed falling among the thorns refers to someone who hears the word, but the worries of this life and the deceitfulness of wealth choke the word, making it unfruitful."

This explanation lists two main distractions to proper depth: *worry* and *wealth*. While each is a sermon in itself, notice that both come from a lack of trust in God's leading or provision.

When fear and worry become so big they drive out all else, they become weeds within our hearts. They choke out fruit. We get obsessed and preoccupied and consumed. What we care about is what we think about, what we spend our time on, what we talk about, what we spend our energy on, what we focus on protecting. This is *what we prioritize*, and if it's not depth in faith, then our faith is suffocated.

Finally we have the seed on good soil. What distinguishes this good ground from the rest is, in a word, *fruitfulness*. It produces the kind of fruit that Galatians 5 tells us we ought to see in a mature Christian: love, joy, peace, patience, kindness, goodness, faithfulness, gentleness, and self-control (vv. 22–23).

No soil is impervious to drought or weeds or malnourishment. Jesus did not say that this good ground has no stones in it, or no thorns, or that the sun will not beat down on it, but only that it is fruitful in the real, hard world.

Where there is fruit, there is the reign of God. Anytime you demonstrate kindness, there is fruit. When you show joy in the face of struggle, there is fruit. If you are gentle when you could be harsh, there is fruit. When we are generous, selfless, good, loving, self-controlled: fruit, fruit, and more fruit.

SO WHAT'S NEXT?

I decided a long time ago that my lot in life was to *become*. What I mean by that is I recognize that I have yet to arrive—and simply won't until Jesus returns. I am consistently *becoming* the man God wants me to be. He knows where I am and loves me regardless. I won't beat myself up when I'm not as far along as I should be. I won't compare myself to others. I'll seek to see myself as God sees me: his child. I'm not going to fall prey to false condemnation and guilt. I won't be shamed. I know from Scripture that both are lies from the Enemy.

Instead, I will continue to fight for depth, because deeper faith leads to fuller life. I know I won't find contentment and peace in the shallows. They are deceptive and lead only to disappointment and confusion. No, I will focus, rather, on a few key areas of faith in which I've only skimmed the surface over the years.

Finding depth in those areas is turning out to be an absolute game changer for me. Come to find out, many well-intentioned believers hold myopic views on some of the same issues. So, for the remainder of the book, we'll dig into those areas.

Bottom line is that we're all in this together. We're craving depth. We're craving rootedness. Let's begin our journey.

DISCUSSION QUESTIONS

1. In the story of the woman caught in adultery, with whom do you identify most: the teachers of the law, the onlookers, or the woman herself? Why?

2. Has anyone ever been an advocate for you when you didn't deserve it? What did that feel like? How did that change the way you viewed that person?

3. In what areas are you most likely to be "at risk" of becoming like the "religious" teachers of the law?

4. Have you ever unknowingly judged or accused others because you were defending a truth you believed in? Explain.

5. How is *learning to descend* a spiritual discipline? What other places in the Bible do you see this truth lived out?

6. Have you added a Bible study or small group to your schedule, hoping for more depth, but only discovered you were spread too thin? Was the problem you or the added study? Explain.

7. In the first chapter we discussed three kinds of "depth" we typically crave: depth in understanding, depth in

---

relationships, and depth in spirit. Which do you lack the most? What are you doing or can you do to address this imbalance?

8. What does your daily calendar say about your spiritual depth?

9. Which of the four soils best describes where you are now?

10. Have you ever been more than one soil at one time? Explain your answer.

PART I

THE GOSPEL
IN US

CHAPTER 2

A BIGGER GOSPEL

"For whoever wants to save their life will
lose it, but whoever loses their life for me
and for the gospel will save it."

—MARK 8:35

THINGS CHANGE OVER the years. That said, it's not always the thing itself that changes as much as it's us. I remember driving back to Colorado for the first time as an adult. The house I grew up in, my high school, and even the town seemed smaller than I remembered. The mountains, however, seemed bigger than life. I was actually in awe seeing them again.

The mountains, obviously, hadn't grown. Why had my view of them changed so drastically? Maybe I had grown numb to them over the years as a child. Maybe a more traveled perspective helped me appreciate their uniqueness. Or maybe that's just what happens when you live in Texas. The Texas hill country doesn't quite compare to the Rocky Mountains.

Likewise, our faith changes as we grow. Some things that used to be a big deal to me no longer are. Thank goodness. Many things, I know, stay the same, but it's the gospel that continues to grow in my mind. It's the gospel that seems most like those mountains.

The gospel doesn't actually change. We do. Our perspectives naturally shift with life experience, they shift with maturity, and they shift when we return with a greater desire for truth. But of all the reasons for change, mine changed the most after a desperate prayer on an international flight.

JET-PLANE PRAYER

Several years ago, I boarded a 737 headed for Ethiopia. It was my first time on an overseas mission trip. I had been invited to join a handful of leaders who were at the top of their fields: a vice president of a major software company, the president of a record label and publishing company, a denominational leader, a megachurch pastor, and a couple of nonprofit leaders.

As the wheels left the tarmac, I came to a startling realization: I didn't want to go.

It wasn't a fear of flying, and it wasn't necessarily that I had something more pressing to attend to. In a moment of clarity, I realized that I didn't quite understand or affirm the reason we were going.

Why were we going to Africa?

We were planting trees. For Jesus.

The invitation had come from my friend Steve Fitch, founder of the Eden Projects. I wasn't invited because I had anything to add to the conversation. I was invited because Steve had something he wanted me to see. Eden had multiple reforestation sites in Ethiopia in areas stripped by generations of people using the trees to sell in the market, cook with, and heat their homes. Some regions had become so barren that the wildlife had left and the soil had lost its fertility. Worse, with the lack of underbrush and a healthy root system, the runoff from the escarpment and hillsides had created massive erosion gorges that were not only destroying the land and the lake below, but were creating environmental refugees. These people had nothing but their land and no place to go to if it was taken away from them. Deforestation was destroying communities.

Among other things, Eden focuses first on hiring people from the community to plant seedlings, nurture their growth, and then transplant them on erosion sites. The goal is job creation, environmental care, and community development.

So here was my problem: I was pretty conservative about everything. I grew up believing that anything to do with social action was most likely a departure from the gospel. While I didn't fully understand the historical social gospel that my elder generation seemed to fear, I knew it was off base.

Not only that, my faith had pretty much been consumed by serving saved people, blessing blessed people, and feeling sorry for lost people. I never considered creation care, social enterprise, or community development that important or relevant to me. While it seemed like good and necessary humanitarian work for others, it didn't seem applicable to my faith journey as a church leader and seemed too shortsighted to hold any true eternal significance for others.

I was on that plane because a friend had asked me to go. I agreed because God had recently taken me on my own journey that forever changed how I "do" church. My wife, Jen, and I had spent the past few years learning to serve, engaging issues of poverty, homelessness, and helplessness. It may have seemed as though this trip would be in my lane. I thought I had broken through to see things through a new lens; certainly I was more open-minded than before. Yet it still seemed like a stretch to make a connection between planting trees and the gospel.

My issue wasn't whether or not this was good and necessary work. It was that I couldn't quite tell from the trip agenda when we were going to share the good news. It was all good, but how were we going to tell people about Jesus?

Signs of my angst were obvious. Just a week before the trip, a friend had asked why I was going. I didn't say we were planting trees. I told him we were doing some community development work with local pastors. That was true, kind of, but not very specific. I just couldn't bring myself to say we were planting trees. I couldn't find the words.

Honestly, I was a little nervous I was taking it too far. I couldn't help but wonder if I was on a slippery slope that would land me somewhere in a commune where I'd sell all my possessions and fully depart from my conservative theological roots.

So I prayed.

"God, I'm sorry. I'm trying, but I just don't get it. I don't want to be on this plane. I feel like I'm wasting time and money. If this is important to you, will you please overcome my ignorance, doubt, and blindness? Will you connect the dots and show me what I'm missing? Amen."

That was it. A short, honest prayer.

The moment I opened my eyes, someone tapped me on my right shoulder. I turned to see a well-dressed, thirtysomething Ethiopian man with an inquiring look on his face.

"Why are you going to Ethiopia?" he said with a heavy accent.

My mind rushed. *Do I tell him community development? Do I tell him the pastor stuff? Do I tell him . . .*

"We're planting trees," I blurted out.

Not sure why I said that. It was like a confession. Then I just stared at him, bracing for his response. *What is he thinking? What am I thinking? Who do I think I am? I don't even know what I'm doing . . . Who am I to come to another country and think I'm going to make a difference? His country. I'm not even sure I should be doing this.*

Silence.

Then an elderly Ethiopian woman leaned over to the man and spoke to him in Amharic. He responded back in Amharic. And she began to wail.

I don't mean cry a little. I mean *wail.* She stood up, waving her hands in the air, continuing to speak Amharic loudly. Everyone in that section of the plane could hear her.

"What's going on?" I asked.

"My mother asked me why you were going to Ethiopia."

"What did you tell her?"

"I told her you were going to plant trees."

I knew it. I totally knew it. I hadn't even touched the ground yet, and I'd offended this woman. She was probably praying for my soul, that I would stop being so distracted by the things of this world and focus more on a true gospel.

"What is she saying?"

"My mother is saying that for thirty-eight years she has been praying that God would forgive them for stripping their land and to please send someone to plant trees."

I turned to try and communicate with the woman somehow, to let her know that it wasn't really me doing the work . . . I might plant a few . . . but it was this organization. But before I could say a word, she slapped her hand on my head, closed her eyes, and began to pray for me. Standing in the middle of the airplane. As loud as possible between her wailing . . . she prayed for me.

Unreal.

In a moment I had gained a new appreciation for what it meant to offer hope through engaging need. My heart broke for her. And I was incredibly humbled. Embarrassed a little. Many people had come before me to help with this need. Reforestation in Africa was obviously not starting with me. To this point I had done nothing outside of some financial support to the organization through our church. But it made no difference to this woman. No way around it. Anyone planting trees in Ethiopia was good news to her.

And I saw it even more clearly on the ground. I saw trees planted, jobs created, schools funded, and churches started. Hundreds of people were coming to faith, and entire communities were renewed with hope by the work of the gospel.

My gospel was too small.

I've learned a lot since then. First and foremost, as beautiful as it was, my gospel experience was fairly one-dimensional. Therefore, it had remained fairly one-dimensional. Our view of the gospel impacts everything, and I've come to realize that most of my spiritual shortfalls, my angst with church culture, and my struggles to find true significance in the kingdom come from that same myopic place.

A LIMITED PERSPECTIVE

There's something unique about how we first encounter Jesus. That form, whatever it may be, tends to hold a special place in our lives. It seems pure, and rightfully so. It's the place in which we first experienced hope. This space, however, can quickly become the thing we are most likely to start defending, even if there comes a time when we need to reevaluate its effectiveness. It may serve us best to expand our understanding of the gospel by doing a little introspection. How did you first come to know Jesus?

- Maybe you first heard about Jesus at a revival in a small, traditional church. After fighting with yourself all week, you finally released the death grip on the pew in front of you and made your way to the front to receive Christ.
- Or maybe your mom and dad decided to visit the church that met in the local high school auditorium. It was like no church you had ever seen. The music was amazing, and the pastor made sense. One summer you got saved at youth camp and were baptized that next Sunday.

- Perhaps you grew up in a rough neighborhood or tough family environment where church was never really a part of your life. For years a student mentor at the community center poured into you. He talked about the kingdom of God in ways you'd never heard before. After two years of hanging out and a single prayer, your life was changed forever.

- Maybe you heard about a faith-based nonprofit in your city that focused on helping homeless families. One evening after seeing yet another family rescued from the streets, it became clear that it was because of Christ. In a moment of solitude in your own bedroom, you realized you were just like that family in need, completely spiritually impoverished, and asked Jesus to save you.

- Or perhaps you experienced Christ for the first time at a recovery group. It was a place of vulnerability and trust and talk of the hope of a renewed life. Maybe it wasn't the idea of Christ that initially drew you, but you quickly found out that he was at the center of this group. And you needed him.

The way we first encountered Jesus will most naturally seem like the purest form of the gospel. It's the lens through which we will likely view the gospel most clearly. This is the lane in which we'll most intuitively continue. But it's a beginner's lane. While God uses our experiences to shape us into who we're becoming, it's not until we see how our story intersects with others that our gospel will begin to grow. That lane is supposed to widen.

The word *gospel* means "good news." Jesus becoming flesh

was certainly the beginning of good news for us, but it didn't end with his incarnation. The power was in his life and his death. Jesus applied who he was and what he knew by focusing his efforts and digging into the lives of others. He injected himself into their stories, often with a deliberate attempt to reposition himself. He knelt to be eye to eye with the woman caught in adultery and became her advocate. He rerouted his journey through Samaria to meet the woman at the well and spoke truth. He invited himself to dinner at Zacchaeus's house and became his friend.

Jesus became good news by repositioning himself toward others. His standard mode of operation was to meet people where they were. At their greatest point of need. This was the gospel as it was intended to be. One that transcends culture. Juxtaposed, a gospel that attempts to lure others to reposition themselves toward us is a limited gospel. It seeks to force our story upon others instead of inserting ourselves into their stories. This is the exact opposite of Christ's example. Jesus becoming good news was never limited by context or another's inability to move toward him.

> The way we first encountered Jesus will most naturally seem like the purest form of the gospel.

I believe this to be one of the root issues in church culture today. We limit the gospel by how we define it. We try to control it by making it too much about us, our form, and our function. Thus, what we're hoping to embody lacks perspective and empathy, the very things that make the gospel good news to others. The result? We're ineffective. Others get frustrated. We get confused. And the gospel seems to lack power. This isn't the way it was meant to be. Yet it's how so many of us live.

Jesus embraced multiple ways of becoming good news to others. He always spoke in ways they understood, he empathized with them, and he started by engaging their greatest need. This was a posture that was foundational to the early church. Paul wrote about it in his first letter to Corinth:

> To the Jews I became like a Jew, to win the Jews. To those under the law I became like one under the law (though I myself am not under the law), so as to win those under the law. To those not having the law I became like one not having the law (though I am not free from God's law but am under Christ's law), so as to win those not having the law. To the weak I became weak, to win the weak. I have become all things to all people so that by all possible means I might save some. I do all this for the sake of the gospel, that I may share in its blessings. (1 Corinthians 9:20–23)

Earlier I mentioned five different environments in which one might first experience Christ. In these examples we can see at least three different kinds of first encounters. The first starts directly by engaging spiritual need, the second starts at relational need, and the third starts by addressing physical need. Jesus certainly understood this variety of approaches.

Aside from the cross, no single act fully defined Jesus. He fed the hungry, he healed the sick, and he raised the dead. He brought dignity to the broken, became a friend to the outcast, and touched the untouchable. He poured into the lives of a renegade group of disciples and shared Passover with his betrayer the very night he was betrayed. Somehow, in each of these moments, the gospel is revealed. People are given hope, sin is exposed, and we are drawn toward a Savior who loves like no other.

The gospel is no less evident and no less powerful in one environment than another. In fact, it only becomes most powerful when it's personalized. God knows us better than we know ourselves. By his amazing design, the gospel meets us where we are. Jesus meets us at our greatest deficiency and brings us to his greatest sufficiency.

We need to consider a bigger gospel. One that builds on rather than restricts us to what we first experienced. Not only to open our eyes to God's greater redemptive plan, but also to allow us to experience all God has in store for our lives. This will help us to see ourselves as Christ sees us, to see others as Christ sees them, and to become better stewards of the gospel.

A BIGGER GOSPEL

The gospel is plural. When we view it as singular, we limit how we view God working in our world and minimize the opportunities that are in front of us. This only increases frustration and makes us less effective for the kingdom.

This is not a new concept to believers. God himself is plural. Scripture is clear that God is three in one. The Father is fully God, the Son is fully God, and the Holy Spirit is fully God. At times we see, hear, and learn about the Father at work in Scripture. At times we see, hear, and learn about the Son at work. And at times we see, hear, and learn about the Holy Spirit at work. Each is God. Each is manifested and works in different ways.

I think Tim Keller said it best: "Like God, the gospel is both one and more than that."[1] The gospel saves, transforms, and renews. The same gospel that saves you is at work today in restoring all creation. It's working in your life, your home, and in your church, just as it is in other people's lives, homes, and churches.

A firm foundation starts with a deeper understanding of the gospel's plurality. Let's take a moment to dig into three very important ways in which the gospel is at work.

Humble Beginnings: Salvation

The gospel is most certainly doctrinal. It's a gospel that saves. The doctrine of salvation is the good news that God so loved the world that he gave his only Son. Through him we are declared innocent, and through him we gain eternal life. A gospel that saves makes us sons and daughters of the King. The good news is that Jesus came not for the righteous but for sinners, and that salvation is available to all of us.

"Everyone who calls on the name of the Lord will be saved" (Romans 10:13).

There's a lot of confusion in the world about how someone really gets saved. The arguments are most often about the method, not the doctrine of salvation itself. Did we walk the aisle? Did we say the prayer? Did we stand in front of the church and make a "public profession"?

In the midst of all this confusion, we can be confident in a few truths:

First, regardless of how you came to faith, it's clear that it only takes a simple, childlike faith in Christ to be saved. It doesn't require a seminary degree. We just need to understand our inability and Christ's sufficiency. I'm not saying that it's not complex; I'm just saying that the gospel's invitation requires confession and acceptance, not a full comprehension of its kingdom implications. Many of those things are spiritually discerned. It's the gospel's work in us as we continue our journey that brings us to a greater understanding of the kingdom.

The gospel's first work is to save you. This is important to understand. As a child and young adult, I probably asked Jesus to save me ten thousand times. I wasn't sure at the time why I lacked spiritual security, but I know now that I was placing my confidence in my (lame) behavior instead of my identity in Christ. I had allowed my inability to overshadow Christ's ability. That led to a spiritual prison of sorts. I didn't even realize I was on a hamster wheel of faith completely consumed with *me*. Every day, every action, every thought related to faith made me think about myself and my failures. Maybe the same is true for you.

Yet, the Bible says that you can "*know* that you have eternal life" (1 John 5:13, emphasis added). And you can trust that "it is for freedom that Christ has set us free" (Galatians 5:1). You can have confidence knowing that first time you believed and truly confessed Jesus as Lord, he saved you. We have a real enemy who doesn't want us to have that confidence. He knows that if he can keep us consumed with and worried about whether or not we're truly saved, we'll never move on to doing good stuff for the kingdom. God wants you to know.

It's critical, as believers, that we move beyond our doubt into confidence. We can trust the good news:

> If you declare with your mouth, "Jesus is Lord," and believe in your heart that God raised him from the dead, you will be saved. For it is with your heart that you believe and are justified, and it is with your mouth that you profess your faith and are saved. (Romans 10:9–10)

The second thing we can have confidence in is that our salvation is not based on our behavior or our ability to save ourselves, but upon Christ and his sacrifice. There is nothing we can do to earn our own salvation. Thus, there is nothing we can do to lose our salvation. The good news is that we can stop stressing, performing, and worrying. Jesus himself invites us to "take my yoke upon you and learn from me, for I am gentle and humble in heart, and you will find rest for your souls" (Matthew 11:29).

It's an exchange of sorts. His perfection for our sin. Baffles me when I think about it. But that's the God I see in the Bible. That's the good news.

The third point of confidence is that the gospel's work is not complete at salvation. God has something more in mind for each of us. The gospel has work to do. And what God has started in you will be finished. In fact, this was Paul's greatest encouragement to the church: "[Be] confident of this, that he who began a good work in you will carry it on to completion until the day of Christ Jesus" (Philippians 1:3, 6).

I grew up thinking that once I was saved the major work was

done. It was the golden ticket. After that I just needed to hold on until Jesus came back. It was kind of like buying fire insurance. Make the monthly payments, don't sin too much, and squeak my way into heaven.

This view was evident in how I lived my faith. While it started with zeal, eventually my attempt to be a part of the church became a checklist, people became projects, and my growth became stagnant. It rarely crossed my mind that the good news of our salvation had some continued work to do in me.

This led to a pretty miserable existence. Guilt became my main spiritual motivator. I cared more about what others thought of me than what God thought of me. I held on to hope but lost the joy of my salvation. Maybe you can relate, and the gospel just doesn't seem like good news anymore. Perhaps you're stuck because your gospel is too small. Here's some good news . . . there's more gospel ahead.

Everything Changes: Transformation

The gospel's work does not end at our salvation. That's where it begins. The gospel transforms. As we learn to trust the gospel that saves, the gospel that transforms takes us on the adventure of aligning our thoughts and desires with the mind and heart of Christ. It helps us see a better way and sheds light on opportunities to choose his way over our ways. Any realm in our lives where we choose the way of Jesus is the result of a transforming gospel.

In the second chapter of Philippians, Paul wrote, "Work out your salvation with fear and trembling, for it is God who works in you to will and to act in order to fulfill his good purpose"

(vv. 12–13). Simply put, transformation is the lifelong work of the gospel in us in every way. Nothing is left untouched. Once we truly find our identity in Christ, the gospel begins to work, transforming our hearts and minds. We're given a new way to see the world, a new personal scorecard with greater reward, and a new and more fulfilling mission. The gospel becomes an ever-refining lens that clarifies our way. It brings significance to every breath and sheds light in the darkest places. Every moment becomes a learning moment, an opportunity, or an example of the gospel at work.

The gospel doesn't just change our actions; it changes our hearts and minds. It changes the motivation behind our actions. God doesn't want us to live for him and others begrudgingly. He wants to change what we desire, so that when we choose his ways over ours, it breathes life into our journey, so that our greatest fulfillment comes from walking in his footsteps. He wants to make us more like Jesus.

A limited gospel makes life change a discipline. The true gospel changes our heart's desire to live like Christ. It changes our perspective. It's not the other way around. We don't change on our own power hoping to see a glimpse of the gospel. This is a massive paradigm shift for many. A necessary shift.

We don't just take up the cause of the orphan or fight human trafficking because we're supposed to; we do these things as a result of the gospel giving us a heart for justice. We don't extend mercy to others because God said we have to forgive others; we extend mercy because we have learned to love mercy. There's a point where we stop going to church because of guilt and we actually begin to love worshipping God, learning his Word, and being a part of the body of Christ. People stop annoying you because you see their brokenness and identify it with your brokenness. You do things and have thoughts you never imagined you'd have. Why? You're being transformed.

A Fresh Beginning: Restoration

Not long ago, Jen and I considered buying a hundred-year-old farmhouse in old-town Buda, Texas. At the time, it seemed like the perfect renovation project for us. It was situated on a beautiful lot with twelve pecan trees and was in the exact part of town we hoped for. It suited our family perfectly in every way—everything, that is, except the house itself.

The house was rundown and tired.

While the exterior held its original charm, the inside had obvious "updates" and additions that screamed of decades past. Each addition was like another domino falling away from its historical allure, each one making it less likely to suit the Hatmaker family.

But we didn't consider it based on its current condition; we bought it for its potential. We knew what we could make of it. So we bought the home, sold our old one, and moved in as is.

We lived in the house during the demolition and deconstruction. That was definitely the most difficult part. There were times without heat, water, a living room, and the entire time we were without a kitchen. Everything that made home comfortable was displaced during that time. Construction dust and debris were everywhere, and nothing seemed to be going as planned.

But there was a moment when the old drywall was ripped away, the walls were gone, and we could finally see the original studs that held the house together. What we saw was a solid house. The craftsmanship was amazing. For the first time we could see what we were really working with, and hope was restored that it was worth the sacrifice.

Then the fun began. Our plan was to restore the home to suit our family, adding a bedroom here, a bathroom there, repurposing everything we could. Each room had our personal touch, design, and feel. It wasn't exactly like the home was when it was first built. Instead, it was better than new, because it was built with my family in mind.

We've discussed in depth how the gospel works to save and transform, but it doesn't stop there. The gospel also restores and makes all things new. The good news of the kingdom is that God has this amazing plan outlined from Genesis to Revelation to restore all of creation. That includes us. The invitation is to find our story as a part of his greater story.

Once we find our identity in a gospel that saves, the Spirit moves in and starts making changes. Transformation often starts with some deconstruction, stripping away the years of short-sighted renovations, worn-down materials, and mistakes. From there the gospel works in us to take what was broken and restore it, redeeming lost moments, broken opportunities, failures, and shortcomings.

"The God of all grace, who has called you to his eternal glory in Christ, will himself restore, confirm, strengthen, and establish you" (1 Peter 5:10).

Restoration is a hard concept to absorb with a finite mind, because it's a concept that is realized in eternity. We are restored in many different ways. Each way brings glory to God, offers hope to the believer, and announces the new way of the king-dom. Living a gospel-centered life is *the* difference between a constantly yearning faith and a consistently fulfilled faith.

Simply put, Jesus is in the business of putting broken things back together. That's the good news. When we trust the gospel, Jesus redeems our past, our present, and our future by restoring our souls, our stories, and our hope.

I don't know what's going through your mind as you read this. Each of us comes from a different background, with different experi-ences, different failures, and different successes. Some things will resonate with you, and others might rub you wrong. But if you do anything, my prayer is that you'll consider a gospel that is not limited by us, our think-ing, or even our dreams.

> Living a gospel-centered life is *the* difference between a constantly yearning faith and a consistently fulfilled faith.

We can't out-dream God. His desire is that we would each live our greatest story. A story that only he could author.

I pray that you'll pursue and receive a gospel that heals your every wound, allowing it to comfort you in your most broken places. I pray that it's your greatest hope, that it becomes your greatest source of peace, and that when in doubt, you'll choose to trust that Christ can accomplish in you and through you any-thing he wills. What he has begun in you, he will complete.

I also pray that you'll apply the same gospel to how you view others. That you'll live by the standards that align with the king-dom Jesus ushered in. That whenever you feel spiritual pride and judgment, you'll replace it with humility and grace. That you'll pursue truth, but never go through, around, or over people to get there. That you'll be an advocate for others, kneel in the dirt to extend dignity, and become a friend to the outcast. That you'll not only receive the gospel, but you'll embody it as you seek to be more like Jesus.

"A new command I give you," Jesus said. "Love one another. As I have loved you, so you must love one another. By this everyone will know that you are my disciples, if you love one another" (John 13:34–35).

DISCUSSION QUESTIONS

1. Have you ever had an experience that challenged or shifted your view of the gospel? Share your experience with the group. How has that experience changed you? How has it influenced your view of church?

2. In what ways have your understanding of the gospel's work in or through you been limited? Why do you think that is? How has that impacted your journey?

3. Brandon shared several different scenarios of first encounters with Christ. Which environment do you identify with the most?

4. How has that experience formed your current view of the gospel? How has it changed?

5. Has your experience ever caused you to question the validity of someone else's experience? Why?

6. In this chapter, Brandon discussed how the gospel saves, transforms, and restores. If each action were on a timeline, where would you place yourself at this moment?

7. Which of the three dimensions of the gospel do you least understand? Why do you think that is?

8. Which of the three dimensions do you most naturally trust? Why? What can you do to press into or consider the other areas more deeply?

9. How does your view of the gospel inform how you view yourself? How does it inform how you view God?

10. In what ways should a holistic gospel shape the way you live out biblical community? How would you expect that to change your community?

CHAPTER 3

A NEW IDENTITY

See what great love the Father has lavished
on us, that we should be called children
of God! And that is what we are!

—1 JOHN 3:1

I GREW UP living two different lives.

Both of my lives seemed incredibly real and part of who I was. It wasn't that I wanted to live two lives. They both felt necessary to complete me, yet also seemed so independent of each other, as if there was no point where the two could merge with any type of authenticity.

One of my lives really loved Jesus. I attended church every Sunday with my mom and sister, youth group every Wednesday, and church camp every summer. I had spiritual experiences and seasons that were incredibly fulfilling. I really liked this me, but this me didn't seem capable of surviving in the real world. It was idealistic but felt impractical. I wasn't sure I could keep it up. And it didn't seem to translate well into my everyday life.

The other me wished he could stay home on Sundays to watch football. This me loved being a teenager and everything that went with it. It felt as if this was most likely the real me, the one that controlled my attitudes, my relationships, and my dreams. Although the other me consumed my mind the majority of the time, this one controlled my actions. This me knew about the other me and felt guilty all the time.

I was spiritually conflicted. But I really didn't know how to get from where I was to where I was supposed to be.

It got worse when I went to college.

I never dreamed of attending a Christian college, but in the summer of 1990, I loaded down my car with everything I owned and made the transition from high school senior in Colorado to incoming freshman at Oklahoma Baptist University. It was a culture shock. I had never lived in the *Bible Belt*, much less gone to a Christian school. The first week felt more like church camp than it did college.

I knew right away which me needed to show up. This me, however, didn't have the Guess jean shorts and polo shirts everyone else seemed to have. I didn't know who Michael W. Smith was, or DC Talk. My pocket-sized New Testament was difficult enough to read, much less big enough to highlight all my favorite verses and take notes in the margins. I couldn't recite the books of the Bible. And apparently it wasn't cool anymore to cuss.

Fake it till you make it, though, right?

And I did. I fit in with the best of them. I portrayed myself as a good, mature, Christian college boy to the girls I dated, I went to all the campus Bible studies and Christian clubs, and I joined in on the Christian conversations the best I could in the student lounge. I wanted it to be real . . . but I was faking it. On the outside I looked like everyone else, but on the inside I was insecure, lonely, and felt like a fraud. My charade lasted about six months before the old me took over.

This became a cycle over the next few years. Many times I found myself trying to be and eventually pretending to be something better, more spiritual, more Christian than I really was, but inevitably reverting to the comforts of the old me. I often disappointed those around me. Along with this came spiritual shame and false condemnation. Since no one really knew what was going on in my life, no one told me how to deal with it. Even as an adult, later on, I lived in spiritual confusion from time to time. It wasn't as noticeable as when I was younger, but there were certainly seasons when I just didn't feel as transformed or spiritually disciplined as I was acting.

As I matured physically and emotionally, I began to realize what was happening spiritually. I was in a battle for my identity, and I had a real enemy contending for who I was. While it was natural that the new me did not yet feel as authentic as the old me, that realization wasn't intuitive. That was the most difficult part for me, because I have a deep desire to be honest, to be authentic, and it didn't feel authentic.

Two things I've learned since then: First, I've realized that I spent the majority of my early Christian years falsely equating spiritual health with attendance at church programs. Not only does this not add up, but it's not biblical. True Christianity is lived along the way, between the church services and Bible studies. Programs and events on the church campus are a significant part of the Christian journey, but they do not define us. The purest of moments communing with God and other believers, whether in exaltation or confession, are mostly *responses* to who we are, not the other way around.

> **True Christianity is lived along the way, between the church services and Bible studies.**

Second, we are never more the real us than when we are closest to Christ. While I was more accustomed to the old me because it had defined the majority of my life, *the old me is not the real me.* It's a lie. The old me was the broken version of who I was before Christ. It was broken me. The real me is being made new by the gospel. It's the *me* that God sees, and the one that matters most.

After all these years, the old me still contends for my identity. It's frustrating at times. I have to deny myself daily. But that's to be expected. Jesus taught that it's a part of the journey. It's when I forget this truth that I become most vulnerable to slipping back into old habits and practices.

That said, I would say that I'm no longer consumed with or defined by how others view me or by my failures. In fact, because I am a fairly unconventional church leader who rides a Harley, has tattoos, and typically hangs out with a pretty rough crowd, there are those who question my identity and agenda. None of us are without critics. But those people don't define me.

What defines me is that I'm a child of God. Regardless of how I look on the outside or how I spend my time. I am a sinner saved by grace, assured of who I am in Christ.

OVERCOMING FEAR AND SHAME

One of the things important for any believer to understand is how fear and shame impact our identity. Whether I could verbalize it or not growing up, too often I envisioned God sitting on the clouds, waiting to throw thunderbolts at my every sin. I looked at my own shortfalls and could only imagine a God who was frustrated with humanity, especially my humanity. Why wouldn't he punish me or be disappointed in me? That would make total sense.

It's uncanny how we allow fear to seep in. Fear of failure. Fear of change. Fear of being found out. Fear of being misunderstood. Fear of judgment.

Fear leads to shame. Shame causes us to doubt. We begin to doubt God's love and we begin to doubt God's grace. Ultimately, we begin to doubt the ability of the gospel to work in our lives.

It's good to remember that God is no stranger to the response of fear. Throughout Scripture, whenever God revealed himself directly to his people, either as an angel of the Lord or as Jesus himself, the people's first reaction was terror. There was something about experiencing the true presence of God that was incredibly revealing and confronting.

God's response every time: "Fear not."

From there he would explain why. Fear not, for I am with you. Fear not, for I am your God. Fear not, for I will strengthen you and I will help you. Fear not, for I bring you great news. (See Isaiah 41:10, 13; 43:5 NKJV; Luke 2:10 KJV.)

In order to take our gospel identity seriously, we have to stop fearing our inabilities and start believing in God's ability, that he is with us and that he is for us, and that his view of us and our circumstances is more expansive than ours. This has nothing to do with what we can accomplish; it has everything to do with what we can surrender. Our fear is unnecessary and our shame is unfounded.

It wasn't until a handful of years ago that I fully embraced the reality that God saw me differently than I saw myself. I always felt as if God were disappointed, and that, compared to others, I was consistently failing him. Shame seemed to define me. Because of this, I struggled with the fear that I wasn't doing enough and began to value works over pursuing and embracing truth.

Scripture never points us to *more works* as a means to earn God's approval. Ever. When we place our hope in our spiritual achievement, we make our faith more about us than about God. When we do so, we are attempting to change the gospel to fit our lives instead of allowing the truth of the gospel to change our lives. The focus becomes what we do rather than who we are because of Jesus and who he is.

Scripture is clear to define God with one word: *love* (1 John 4:8). While he is indeed Creator, Sustainer, and Judge, love is both the infrastructure and the fuel for each of his other characteristics. God's nature is holy and righteous. We know this. It's part of the reason we tend to fear God's judgment.

But in God's love, he poured out his full wrath on the cross. There is none left. Jesus bore it all. Thus, our identity does not start with us; it starts with Christ.

God presented Christ as a sacrifice of atonement, through the shedding of his blood—to be received by faith. He did this to demonstrate his righteousness, because in his forbearance he had left the sins committed beforehand unpunished—he did it to demonstrate his righteousness at the present time, so as to be just and the one who justifies those who have faith in Jesus. (Romans 3:25–26)

Where does this leave us? Justified by grace. That's how God views us. He declares us innocent. It's a new day and a new *me*. We must first believe this truth in order to live this truth.

Regardless of our failures, Christ levels the playing field at the foot of the cross. Our starting point is truly, "Not guilty." Ponder that for a moment. This is our reality. Anything else is a lie. The truth of our identity is how God sees us. Here's what Scripture says about us:

- We are saved by grace: "God saved you by his grace when you believed. And you can't take credit for this; it is a gift from God" (Ephesians 2:8 NLT).
- We are new creations: "Anyone who belongs to Christ has become a new person. The old life is gone; a new life has begun!" (2 Corinthians 5:17 NLT).
- We are righteous and holy: "Put on the new self, created to be like God in true righteousness and holiness" (Ephesians 4:24).
- We are his messengers of reconciliation: "All this is from God, who reconciled us to himself through Christ and gave us the ministry of reconciliation: that

God was reconciling the world to himself in Christ,
not counting people's sins against them. And he
has committed to us the message of reconciliation"
(2 Corinthians 5:18–19).

It's easy to see how we can wrongly view ourselves in terms of judgment. We are taught to trust that we are justified spiritually—that God declares us innocent because justice was served on the cross—even though we are incredibly guilty. It's hard to absorb this reality, especially when we've lived most of our lives learning to fear the consequences of sin. But this is what God sees when he looks at us: Forgiven. Clean. Righteous. Worthy. And when we understand this, when we finally, truly believe it, our attitudes and behaviors change. We will find ourselves wrapped in the gospel that transforms. The result is true appreciation, humility, and life-altering gratitude.

I like how Jeff Vandersteldt put it in an article he wrote for the Gospel Coalition's blog:

Whenever the people in the churches that Paul influenced went sideways, he didn't just confront their wrongdoing and tell them what to do. He started by reminding them of who God is, what God had done for them in Jesus, and who they were in light of that truth. Then he reminded them of how believing the truth about the gospel and their new identity would lead them to different behavior. Paul knew that all of our behaviors result from what we believe about who God is as revealed through what God does, leading to what we believe about who we are. God's work in Jesus Christ grants us a whole new identity, and this new identity leads to a whole new way of living.[1]

POSITIONS IN CHRIST

So how do we make the journey from confused identity to confidence in Christ? Let's start by taking a moment to consider what exactly it means to be "in Christ."

Jesus' direct promise to us is that if we remain in him, he will remain in us (John 15:4). To remain means to maintain or hold a position. More specifically, it means to abide or to take residence *in* Christ. To do this we need to understand the different positions we have in Christ. It serves us well to know where we stand.

Paul spoke to this in his letter to the Colossians, where he wrote to them about living in freedom from the law and the temptation of a shallow religion. Ironically, he wrote this letter about freedom from prison; he certainly believed that our freedom and fullness in Christ are first and foremost not bound by external circumstance. Let's take a closer look at his words.

> Since, then, you have been raised with Christ, set your hearts on things above, where Christ is seated at the right hand of God. Set your minds on things above, not on earthly things. For you died, and your life is now hidden with Christ in God. When Christ, who is your life, appears, then you also will appear with him in glory. Put to death, therefore, whatever belongs to your earthly nature. (Colossians 3:1–5)

Position One: We Died with Christ (Colossians 3:3a)

Paul didn't state that we were numbed to sleep with Christ or temporarily paralyzed with Christ. We died with Christ. More specifically, while the old me may contend for the appearance of life over the new me, God does not acknowledge its existence. It's buried. It is no more.

The only one still acknowledging the old me is me. Sometimes our accusers and our critics will point to our old selves as well, but in Christ, earthly opinion is irrelevant. Scripture makes a bold and clear statement that we need to remember:

> There is now no condemnation for those who are in Christ Jesus, because through Christ Jesus the law of the Spirit who gives life has set you free from the law of sin and death. For what the law was powerless to do because it was weakened by the flesh, God did by sending his own Son in the likeness of sinful flesh to be a sin offering. And so he condemned sin in the flesh, in order that the righteous requirement of the law might be fully met in us, who do not live according to the flesh but according to the Spirit. (Romans 8:1–4)

Position Two: We Are Hidden in Christ (Colossians 3:3b)

In 1995 I boarded a bus headed to basic training for the United States Army. For months I was taught the basic skills necessary for every soldier to survive in a combat situation. I learned everything from hand-to-hand combat and rifle marksmanship to evaluating a casualty and identifying my eight-point grid coordinates on a map by using terrain association. Sounds complicated, but honestly, at this level we weren't really trained to thrive in combat; we were trained to survive.

One of the most important things we learned was the difference between cover and concealment. *Cover* offers physical protection from an opponent's weapon. It's anything that can literally block a bullet. *Concealment* is anything that blocks the opponent's ability to see you. In combat it's critical to know when and how to utilize each. Without them we are left vulnerable and defenseless.

Paul taught that we are in a spiritual war for our identity. In Ephesians 6:12 he reminded us that "our struggle is not against flesh and blood, but against the rulers, against the authorities, against the powers of this dark world and against the spiritual forces of evil in the heavenly realms." Yet, he told the Colossians that since we have died with Christ, we have an additional position in Christ: our life is now *hidden* with Christ in God. Like a treasure hidden in a field for safekeeping, our life is now laid up with God. Our salvation, our future, and our identity are protected. None of them are at risk. This is good news to those of us who consistently return to doubt and false condemnation.

Believer, you are covered and concealed with the blood of Christ. God knows your ugliest details and loves you anyway. In the middle of all our shortcomings, his Son died for us that we might have life. You are the Master's greatest possession, and he has hidden you away for keeps. This is your place. Take heart.

Position Three: We Live in Christ (Colossians 3:4a)

The word *life* in this scripture is the Greek word *zoe*, which refers to all life, both physical and spiritual. All life throughout the universe is derived from and sustained by God's self-existent life, and the Lord intimately shares that gift of life with us.

This life comes with a shared purpose and a shared hope that, unlike worldly standards, does not disqualify based on our past. Its only qualification is the confession of Christ as Lord. It's important we remember this is not a feeling or an emotion; it is a position. Because of the cross, we are God's children. We can have confidence in our life right *now*.

I'm convinced that one of Satan's greatest strategies is to cause believers to live in doubt. When he keeps us confused and insecure, we spend our lives navel-gazing and wondering whether or not we're even saved. It's hard to focus on a new life and mission in Christ when we're worried about the old life that's gone. Fear and shame are strategies of the Enemy. That said, each of us should believe the promise of Scripture, reject spiritual doubt, and live in the freedom and confidence that Christ offers.

Position Four: We Are Raised with Christ and Glorified in Christ (Colossians 3:1, 4b)

In the late 1700s, Charles Wesley wrote the hymn "Hark! The Herald Angels Sing." It's one of my favorite Christmas songs because it reminds us not only how much God loves us but also that the Savior was born with the purpose of changing everything about us. Look at verse 3 (emphasis added):

> Hail the heav'n-born Prince of Peace!
> Hail the Son of Righteousness!

Light and life to all He brings,

Ris'n with healing in His wings:

Mild He lays His glory by,

Born that man no more may die;

Born to raise the sons of earth;

Born to give them second birth.

Paul began Colossians 3 with a statement of fact: you have been raised with Christ (v. 1). Just a few short verses later he completed the thought: you also will appear with him in glory (v. 4). Because of this, we don't have to fear our future and we don't have to fear eternal judgment.

We don't have to be anxious about God's plan for our lives. All we have to know is that if we seek him we'll find him. He's got a plan and he's big enough to let us know what we need to be doing when we need to be doing it. And we don't have to worry about standing before God one day. Instead, we can just do our best to live for him today, knowing that whatever we do, he takes us wherever he goes. We are in Christ, and we are with Christ.

Knowing these things, how should we respond?

Paul's final instruction from our highlighted scripture is to then "put to death . . . whatever belongs to your earthly nature." Ugh. How can we possibly do that? I mean, isn't that the problem in the first place?

Yes. It actually is. But Paul wasn't just writing to tell us our position in Christ and then frustrate us without giving some insight into how this is done. In fact, he was very clear. First of all, knowing our place in Christ gives us the confidence to live as children of God. Children live differently, have a special assurance, and approach the throne knowing their father is for them, not against them. Only heirs to the throne can do what Paul outlined in the first few verses of Colossians 3: "Since, then, you have been raised with Christ, set your hearts on things above, where Christ is, seated at the right hand of God. Set your minds on things above, not on earthly things."

Christ's position at the right hand of God affirms his authority and gives us confidence in the resurrection. Paul's words are a challenge to set our hearts and minds on the supernatural work of the cross. Therein lies our hope. The only way we can effectively find our identity in Christ is to place our hope in the redeeming power that makes us worthy to be raised with him.

> When hope in the gospel becomes our default, we will no longer find our identity in the things of this world; we will find it in Christ alone.

We should consider, reconsider, evaluate, and return, over and over, to hope in Jesus alone. Not in our religious works. Not in our spiritual accomplishments. Not in our earthly positions. *When hope in the gospel becomes our default, we will no longer find our identity in the things of this world; we will find it in Christ alone.*

THE FEELING OF IDENTITY

When he was a toddler, my son Caleb took a headfirst plunge from the barstool in our breakfast room onto the hard tile floor.

There was a split second of silence before the signs of concussion immediately presented.

Knowing good and well what was going on, I picked him up and rushed to the hospital just around the corner from our house.

Caleb was our third kid, but we were rookies to this level of trauma. It was pretty intense there for a while. We worked without success for hours to calm him down enough to do an MRI and make sure everything was okay. The doctor said he had given Caleb enough sedative for a horse, yet he was still running through the halls as if he were at Disneyland. Finally, we just had to take him home and observe him for another forty-eight hours. All throughout the trauma, I had this strange calm about me and knew he'd be okay. Jen was a mess.

Two months later, my daughter Sydney had the first of what became multiple seizures. It was both terrifying and confusing. Away we went to the same hospital, same emergency room, and, ironically, the same bed that Caleb had occupied just a few months earlier.

While I was able to keep calm for Caleb, I was an emotional wreck with Sydney. I couldn't keep it together. In fact, at one point Jen had to tell me to step out of the room as they continued with tests. This time, Jen was the oak. And I was the sap. It was embarrassing.

As I leaned against the wall in the hallway, I began to pray. I was confused and a little embarrassed. How could I be so strong when Caleb was in the emergency room yet so weak when Sydney was there? I didn't love her more or him any less . . . did I?

I'll never forget the comforting response I heard in my mind. *You don't love one of them any more or less. You just love them differently.*

It made so much sense. I did. I did love them differently. I loved to wrestle with my boys, put them in headlocks, and poke them in the ribs. I wanted to throw a football with them and take them hunting. I wanted them to learn from their mistakes, even if it meant some pain along the way.

It was different with my little girl. I wanted to snuggle with her on the couch. I wanted her to know she's beautiful and valued. I wanted to save her from making mistakes. I wanted to shelter her from pain. I wanted her to learn everything the easy way.

Relationships are customized to the individual. One of the big mistakes we make as we seek to understand our identity in Christ is in how we evaluate intimacy with Christ, which doesn't always look the same from person to person. We look at how others pray, journal, and worship and feel inadequate, incapable, or just unspiritual. In error, we sometimes allow the way we *feel* while interacting with Christ to determine our position instead of trusting what Scripture says.

But feelings can be deceiving. And at times our feelings do not represent reality.

For example, for years I struggled with my salvation because I didn't *feel* saved. I wrestled with guilt because I didn't *feel* forgiven or like I was doing enough. I spent years trying to emulate other people's faith. I tried to journal, like Jen does, but I just couldn't. I tried to pray for more than five minutes at a time, but I'd get distracted (or, worse, fall asleep). I tried to be gentle and more sensitive but ended up feeling like a bull in a china shop. Essentially, I was spending more time trying to mimic others than I was trying to find the way I most naturally connected with God.

But on that day, in the emergency room hallway, God spoke loud and clear. He said, *Brandon, stop trying to be someone else. Be you. You and I are gonna wrestle a lot. I'm gonna get you in a headlock, and I'm gonna poke you in the ribs. Every now and then I'll pat you on the back. But I'm also gonna bring you to your knees when you need to be brought down a few notches. At that place we'll probably snuggle a little.*

I found myself in that moment. And it started to make sense for the first time. I realized that I identify with the Jacob of the Bible, who wrestled with God all night and wouldn't let him go until he blessed him. This probably defines my life more than any other story in the Bible. What about you? Maybe you're more like Mary, who adored, or Martha, who served. Maybe you're like Peter, who was incredibly faithful, yet wasn't, yet was, and God used him to start the church we see today. Maybe you're a doubting Thomas. Or maybe you're the Samaritan woman at the well.

I don't know how you interact with God or if you, like me, have been trying to force intimacy in a way that isn't really you. But know this: he will meet you where you really are. He's there in that simple, authentic, vulnerable place where your questions are hard and your words are unrehearsed . . . he's waiting for you, to meet the real you among the muck and the mire. Whoever you are and wherever you are, that's the person Jesus died for and the one he desires to walk with every day.

DISCUSSION QUESTIONS

1. Have you ever pretended to be someone you weren't for the sake of a peer group or others around you? What was going on, and why?
2. We all change as we grow and mature, physically, mentally, and spiritually. Have you ever wrestled with knowing whether the old you or the new you was the real you? Explain.
3. Have you ever thought about this struggle as having an enemy contending for your identity? Why or why not?
4. Have you ever thought about a new and/or emerging identity as the work of the gospel in your life? Why or why not?
5. What has been the most difficult thing for you in finding your identity fully in Christ?
6. Thinking about that most difficult thing, how much do you wrestle with it today?
7. What would Jesus say about that thing that has been so difficult for you?
8. Do you know the gospel changes the way God views you but still struggle to believe it yourself? Why is that? Where do you think that comes from?
9. Have you ever evaluated your spiritual health by church attendance? Why?
10. What role does fear, guilt, or shame play in your search for identity? How does the gospel change how you should view those things?

CHAPTER 4

A DEEPER DISCIPLESHIP

*And I pray that you, being rooted and established
in love, may have power, together with all the
Lord's holy people, to grasp how wide and long
and high and deep is the love of Christ, and to
know this love that surpasses knowledge.*

—EPHESIANS 3:17–19

I JOINED A gym a few weeks ago. I have to admit: it's been a
while. In some ways I surprise myself. In others, not so much.
It's a weird thing when your joints and ligaments hurt more the
next day than your muscles do. At forty-plus, it's just not quite
the same. In the words of Toby Keith, "I ain't as good as I once
was . . . but I'm as good once as I ever was."[1] I wonder if he wrote
that song at the YMCA.

I digress.

You can learn a lot about yourself at the gym. There are few things that will expose your strengths and weaknesses more than working out. I've noticed that if I'm not intentional, I'll spend 90 percent of my time working on strengths and completely ignore my weak spots. It's funny how that works. The things I need to work on the most are the very things I tend to ignore.

It's harder to work on our weaknesses. It hurts more, physically and emotionally. Not only does it feel as if rigor mortis has set in the next day; it takes a little vulnerability and a lot of humility to do military presses with just the bar when the muscle head next to you is stacking on forty-fives.

The thing to realize, though, is that we'll find our greatest gain by working on our weaknesses. It's the pathway to overall health and balance. But it won't happen without self-evaluation, humility, and intentionality. If we don't take a time-out to consider our goals and develop a plan, we'll fail to reach our potential every time. This is true in so many spheres of our lives.

Most of us do church well. We do Bible study well (when we do it). We even hang out with other believers well—we know the rhetoric and have our check boxes. But what we struggle with is . . . well, the other things. We struggle in our neighborhoods. We struggle in our workplaces. We struggle with a lack of transformation. We struggle privately with doubt. Yet, we rarely program space into our calendars for extra reps in these weak areas. Why? Unless there's another Bible study or small group on the topic, most of us don't know where to start.

Over the years, the church has thrived in evangelism and Bible study. I would go so far as to say they have become our strengths. But if we were to define a disciple as one who learns to live out the gospel in all our daily environments, I would argue that they are our weakness. If we were honest, we'd admit that we're better at being and making converts than we are at being and making disciples.

As we grow, our path to discipleship becomes more complex. Our contexts expand, our experiences increase, and our relationships diversify. Applying our faith becomes less predictable, less concrete, and more dependent on understanding our environment. Discerning our context becomes a critical part of the discipleship journey as we transition from learning about faith to living out our faith.

Yet for many of us, our discipleship never leaves the classroom. The hope of the gospel never seems to seep its way into other areas of our lives. We feel powerless and often frustrated. We remain unchanged and can't seem to figure out why.

I would propose that most of our discipleship efforts are good. Great, even. But often myopic. I think we underestimate the spaces in which the active gospel is working in our lives and the context in which it can be expressed. Bottom line, there's more to our discipleship journey than what most of us are experiencing.

This has everything to do with the lenses through which we view discipleship itself. For most of my life I viewed discipleship through the lens of Bible study and Bible study alone. Sure, it had different forms, but ultimately each focused on knowledge and processing new information. This lens makes the assumption that every disciple is living out each truth in his or her individual context but often comes with very little in-the-field-application training.

True discipleship saturates every fiber of our being. It infuses the gospel into each thought and every moment as it molds us into the persons we are becoming. There is no shelf for true discipleship, for it is never to be put away.

With that in mind, let's take a moment to expand our view of discipleship by taking it out of the classroom and adding three lenses through which we can see and learn from a different angle. Let's consider discipleship through the lenses of (1) experiences that transform our hearts, (2) exchanges that transform our minds, and (3) environments that transform our actions. Each of these is critical in the formation of a disciple. Each builds upon the biblical foundation that the gospel saves, transforms, and renews. These are rarely discussed in traditional discipleship models. Yet, each is something that continues to happen along the way every day.

> There is no shelf for true discipleship, for it is never to be put away.

DISCIPLESHIP EXPERIENCES

My friend Alan Graham founded an organization called Mobile Loaves & Fishes (MLF) in 1998. MLF is a nonprofit that started its work by providing free meals, clothing, and other needs to the homeless and working poor of Austin. But it's bigger than that. Their mission statement says it all: "We provide food and clothing and *promote dignity* to our homeless brothers and sisters in need."[2]

Their focus isn't just about what they do; it's *why* and *how* they do it that makes a difference.

One night, I decided to join Alan on a truck run. I met Alan and his team at the commissary, where we loaded down what Alan affectionately calls a "roach coach," a converted food truck filled to the brim with hot coffee, food, blankets, clothing, and other necessities.

Dozens of trucks go out every day of the week for every meal, each with a specific route to strategically cover our city. Ours went to a handful of street corners and underpasses, providing supplies primarily for the homeless community. Our final stop brought us to a weekly-rate motel, home to many who fall into the category of the working poor.

As we neared the motel, Alan began to explain how motel managers often exploit poor families by charging ridiculously high rates for what they offer, knowing the families have no place else to go. They couldn't afford a nightly hotel, and many could not qualify to rent an apartment or home.

He went on to explain that day workers were lucky to make enough to cover the cost of the motel, leaving nothing for necessities, but for many, it was the only option if they needed a place for their families to stay long-term.

Our stop there was important.

We pulled into the courtyard, and it was pretty much how I had envisioned it. There were teenagers in the corner of the parking lot, hanging out like normal teenagers, older men sitting on chairs near their front doors, and children playing on rusted and broken playground equipment on a small plot of trampled grass.

We were swarmed the moment we pulled in. People were smiling. Grateful.

It was a cold night, and the line was moving slowly since we were handing out extra blankets, socks, and a handful of coats, gloves, and hats. We had been there for about ten minutes when a man in line caught my eye. His skin was coarse, and the lines on his face told the story of years of hard work. He was standing silently with his head down, and you could tell he had been crying.

As he made his way to the front and took his first serving of food, I asked him if he needed more. He nodded. When I asked him how much, he replied, "I have three kids."

Socks? Yes.

Blankets? Yes, please.

Coats? Gloves? Hats? Yes. Yes. Yes.

He began to weep.

"Are you okay?" I asked, "Is there anything else I can help you with?"

"I'm good," he replied. "Sorry. I'm just stuck. I make ninety-five dollars a day, and this place costs me eighty-five dollars a night. After work supplies and a bus ride to and from work . . . I've got nothing left over. My kids haven't eaten a full meal for two days."

He continued.

"I don't pray much. But I just asked God, 'If you're real, please help me feed my kids.' I said, 'Amen,' looked out the window, and you guys pulled up."

I felt as if I had a tennis ball in my throat.

There was something about the environment that night that

put me in tune with every face, every name, and every story. With each person I met, there was a misconception, a bias, fear, or insecurity chipped away from my heart.

And while my heart began to break for this man, hearing his story and seeing his humility and appreciation set me back a little. It was like holding a mirror in front of my face, exposing all the excess I had in my life. I take so much for granted. I'm so unthankful. And I have such a small faith.

In just a few moments God had revealed to me that my prayers were immature prayers, my hope was an immature hope, and my heart was not nearly as grateful as I had thought. The Spirit had begun to speak, and I was listening. I couldn't *not* listen. (I know: double negative.) The message was loud and clear.

I knew Alan had overheard my conversation with the man. As we climbed back into the truck, he looked over at me. "Pretty good night, huh, bro?"

"Yeah, it was," I responded. "If something like that happened to me just once a year, it would be enough. It would completely change my outlook on so many levels. How often does that happen?"

The corner of Alan's mouth tilted up in a half-smile. He replied, "Every single time."

Then he asked me a question, "What do you think I'm doing here, Brandon?"

"A lot of things, I guess," I answered. "Feeding the hungry, bringing hope to the hopeless, sharing the gospel in different forms." I knew we weren't solving the global hunger crisis in one night, but we were doing some good. I had a ton of churchy answers I was trying to avoid.

"I'm making disciples," he said. "You see, we're doing a lot of good here. But my job, and yours as a church leader, is to make disciples. My job is to get as many people out of the pews and onto the streets of our city as I can, because I know it'll change them."

This was paradigm-shifting for me. I'd served people before. I'd been on multiple mission trips and served in different environments. But this was different. This was in my hometown on a Tuesday night. It was something profound wrapped in something seemingly simple. Somehow what we had just done shifted my thinking from handing out a sandwich to learning a name, hearing a story, and connecting at the soul level.

And I heard the Spirit whisper, *Remember what you're experiencing. Capture how this feels, and help others feel the same. This is going to change you. It'll change them too.*

I've thought about that night a thousand times since then. It's the moment when I realized for the first time that something was happening all around me that wasn't about me but was changing my heart. After years of checking boxes and hoping for transformation, I could physically feel my heart being reshaped.

Everyday experiences become *discipleship experiences* when we have the right attitude and perspective. Here are a handful of common postures I've noticed are helpful in fostering these moments of transformation:

- When we step into the moment assuming God is already at work. It's easy to serve others with the wrong heart. This is often the fruit of thinking too highly of ourselves and our efforts. Discipleship experiences almost always occur when we recognize where God is already at work, not where he could be with our help.

- When we step into the moment as learners. Pride is blinding. When we inject ourselves into an experience thinking we know everything, we will fail to grow in that moment. When we look for life lessons, we'll almost always find them.
- When we step into the moment viewing others as Christ sees them. Whether it's someone we're serving, someone who lives across the street, or someone we work with, when we see someone as a person with rights, who desires and deserves to be treated with dignity, it will change how we view ourselves. Those we serve are not a "people group," a project, or a target. They are just like me and you.
- When we step into the moment looking for the gospel at work. We know the gospel is at work. Look for it. Don't be passive. Look for the hope of salvation. Look for renewal and transformation. Press into those moments. Help others see them as well. This is where change happens.
- When we step into the moment hoping to encounter Christ. If we schedule our days looking for moments to encounter Christ, we will constantly find ourselves having life-transforming experiences. We can't help but change when we encounter Christ. Take a moment to consider who Christ was and where he'd be found. Emulate him. Would he be in a hurry? What kind of posture would he take?

Notice what's not on this list. There's no "when we step into the moment hoping to fix something." In fact, transformation is most likely to happen when we don't have all the answers or even know what we're doing. It requires a posture of dependency upon Christ and a hope for the gospel at work in *us* just as much as it is in "them."

Disciples learn to capture the moment. They see the supernatural in the common. They don't wait for experiences to come their way; they look for moments already there. Discipleship experiences aren't bound by an encounter with the homeless or the marginalized; they are also captured in a simple conversation with a waitress, a coworker, or a close friend. But they rarely happen without viewing those experiences as opportunities for change.

DISCIPLESHIP EXCHANGES

I've always been enamored with the idea of becoming better. Isn't that our goal in pretty much every pursuit of our lives? Personally we want to be better husbands or wives, fathers or mothers, or friends. Professionally we want to be promoted, which requires us to be better at what we do. We shoot for better grades and hope to improve at our hobbies, run farther in a shorter amount of time, look better, feel better, and accomplish greater things.

These things don't happen by accident. They start with a decision to do whatever it takes to make change a reality. From there it takes hard work and discipline that supports a new way of thinking.

Most of us want to be better followers of Christ than we are. Growing in Christ is a lifelong endeavor. It's a series of exchanges in which we surrender something of ourselves and replace it with something of Christ. It might be the exchange of a possession, an ability or talent, a way of thinking, or even a way of living.

In his letter to the Romans, Paul revealed a different kind of exchange that changes everything. After reminding the Christians in Rome how God made a way so that we might fully comprehend and be recipients of his great mercy (Romans 11:30–32), he continued:

> Therefore, I urge you, brothers and sisters, in view of God's mercy, to offer your bodies as a living sacrifice, holy and pleasing to God—this is your true and proper worship. Do not conform to the pattern of this world, but be transformed by the renewing of your mind. Then you will be able to test and approve what God's will is—his good, pleasing and perfect will. (Romans 12:1–2)

The word *offer* is the Greek word meaning "to present." When used as a verb, it refers to the act of giving oneself, the sacrifice or the offering, back to God. Paul was literally challenging us to give ourselves back to God as a sacrifice. This is something that many of us understand conceptually but few of us live. The idea of offering every thought, intention, hope, and action back to God is foreign to most believers. Parts of us? Yes. All of us? Hard to comprehend. Yet, Paul couldn't have been clearer as to its implications. A measured decision to exchange our everything for God's everything precedes transformation and the ability to desire, see, and live out God's will.

After my sophomore year in college, I realized my life had been off the rails for quite a while. Although I was a Christian, I was miserable. My life was empty, and I desired the Spirit's intervention. It was a time when I surveyed all I had experienced and hoped for and realized all my expectations had fallen short and would never be enough. I considered my life, my failures. I considered my future in Christ. I considered God's mercy. And, to the best of my ability, I offered myself wholly to him.

This was quite possibly the first moment I truly desired his kingdom over mine. In view of God's mercy, it made so much sense.

". . . be transformed by the renewing of your mind."

The words "renewing of your mind" mean to "make new your mind," to change the way you view something. Paul was urging us toward a shift in thinking. He wanted us to change our pursuits by considering God's promises more deeply and to present ourselves completely to him. It's an offer to exchange our will for his.

"Then you will be able to test and approve what God's will is—his good, pleasing and perfect will."

We may have experienced behavioral change in the past, but Scripture is telling us it's after our "presentation" that we will truly begin to be transformed. It begins the moment we fully surrender to the gospel's redemptive power and submit ourselves to the Spirit's work in our lives. It's like a hidden pathway illuminated. And the light at the end of the tunnel is an increasing ability to see God more clearly and understand his ways.

SALVATION → PRESENTATION → TRANSFORMATION

They say hindsight is 20/20. More than twenty years later, I can tell you with all confidence that something happened to me in that moment when I offered myself to God. I can honestly say that this was the point at which the trajectory of my life shifted multiple degrees and I began to view and process things differently. The exchange was real. And it can be for you as well.

What's significant about this exchange is its finality. Before this decision we seem to reserve the right to choose God depending on the situation. That is not a true exchange. We claim we live for him, but it's conditional. There are strings attached. This is often followed by a lack of transformation and clarity about God's will. Frustration ensues. The cycle continues.

To truly present ourselves to God is to give a blanket commitment. It means we choose his ways over our ways before the dilemma begins. This way our decision is no longer about following him in our minds; it's about following through with what we've already determined to be right.

> To truly present ourselves to God is to give a blanket commitment. It means we choose his ways over our ways before the dilemma begins.

It's unconditional discipleship. That's what the original disciples chose when they left their nets by the water and followed Jesus.

When Jesus said, "Whoever eats my flesh and drinks my blood has eternal life" (John 6:54), almost everyone walked away except for his disciples. When Jesus asked them if they wanted to leave, too, Simon Peter simply responded, "Lord, where else would we go?"

They couldn't go back. They had exchanged everything they were for everything Christ was.

DISCIPLESHIP ENVIRONMENTS

A few years ago, Jen and I adopted two amazing kids from Ethiopia, a beautiful little six-year-old girl named Remy and a charming eight-year-old boy named Ben.

Ben had never played organized soccer, but he grew up playing pickup games in Ethiopia. Although it was mid-season when he first came home, one of the first things I did was register him to play at the YMCA. It was a great instructional league that didn't take competition too seriously, so it seemed like a good fit for a kid who had never been on a team.

Just a few weeks after we brought him home, he was invited to suit up and join the team on game day.

Ben had yet to practice with the team, so he sat nervously on the bench as most of the first half ticked away. And then it came. "Ben, you're in on offense."

He didn't really understand what he was told. He just knew his name and went to the area where the coach was pointing. I've never seen a kid smile so much. The anticipation was building for everyone. All the parents and kids cheered for him. It was a beautiful moment.

As the opposing team threw the ball into play, Ben's smile transformed into determination. Something switched. And within one minute Ben had stolen the ball, dribbled the length of the field, and scored his first goal. Then his second. His third. And his fourth. In less than five minutes.

It. Was. Awesome.

After a handful of minutes and a few more goals, Coach put Ben at goalie. It was the only fair thing to do. That became our Saturday routine. Ben would score several goals immediately, then play goalie for the rest of the game.

The next season we took the advice of a few coaches and signed Ben up for a more competitive select league and played him up an age group. While he was definitely the smallest kid on the field, this put him in the middle of the pack in skill. It was perfect for him.

Not only that, but each of these select teams had a professional trainer who worked with the kids on their technique and skill. Something Ben had never been exposed to.

One day after practice, Ben was a bit frustrated because he couldn't kick the ball as hard as the bigger kids. I knew right away it wasn't a strength thing. Ben is incredibly strong. It was a skill thing.

So the next practice, I pulled his coach aside and asked him to work with Ben. I reminded him that while Ben was good at playing soccer, he had never played organized sports or had the instruction other boys had. I hadn't played soccer, so I wasn't much help, but I did recall Coach saying something about a power kick that was a different form from passing. It was something about kicking down on the ball and striking it with the laces instead of the inside of the foot. Since I didn't know what he was talking about, I asked the coach to take a moment to explain to Ben what he meant.

His response? No.

I'm not sure how long I stood there in silence, processing his *no*. But before I could think of an appropriate response, he continued. "We have three drills we're doing today. Each will help him kick the ball with more force. In fact, each one is designed to help him feel something about the way he kicks that he's not doing now. By the end he'll get it."

Then he said something that resonated with me in so many ways.

"There are some things you can't be taught by hearing. Some things you have to *feel* for yourself."

Then the drills began. The first one seemed to frustrate Ben. The second, he began to grin a little bit. And by the third he was hammering the ball into the goal. Ben quickly turned around to make sure I was watching him. His jaw dropped open. His eyes lit up. And he started to jump around, laughing. He got it.

This is exactly what happened to me that night with my friend Alan. He took me out of the church building and placed me in the streets. It was a new environment that he knew would change me. He knew I was going to feel something there that I'd never feel in a Bible study or a retreat. And he was right. He didn't have to say anything. I felt it all.

Discipleship environments take some intentionality. They tend to follow a discipleship exchange and come with a desire for discipleship experiences. These are the places we might avoid if it weren't for the cross. They are the places where we intentionally position ourselves knowing we'll come face-to-face with others in moments that will challenge our status quo.

EMBRACING ENVIRONMENTS

Discipleship is a commitment to the lifelong journey of discovering the heart of Christ and the lifelong calling to be ambassadors of hope and love to a broken world. The Great Commission was permission to be less religious, less arrogant, less anxious, and to become more loving, humble, and peaceful (ah, that sounds nice). It was a challenge to embody good news. It was a calling to find our full identity in Christ through the work of the gospel that makes all things new.

In Matthew 28:19–20 Jesus challenges us, "Therefore go and make disciples of all nations, baptizing them in the name of the Father and of the Son and of the Holy Spirit, and teaching them to obey everything I have commanded you. And surely I am with you always, to the very end of the age."

If you've heard anyone teach this scripture before, you probably know that the phrase "Therefore, go" is most closely translated to mean "As you are going." It implies action. The word *go* literally means "travel" or "journey." It comes from the word *passage.* Jesus' instructions assume that we will continue the apprenticeship model he taught. And just as Ben's soccer coach instructed, we learn best along the way and in different environments. There are opportunities in every town, at any moment, and in any location to apply what we've been learning.

My heart and mind changed through serving those on the

margins. My faith was anemic before this shift in spiritual priorities, even with a firm foundation, so, naturally, I used to think the environment of serving was more important than the others. It's not. It's just different and serves a specific purpose. *How* we serve offers a key clue to *why* life change organically happens in different environments.

Let's take a moment to discuss three kinds of community that have proven to be necessary and transformative "as you are going" environments:

1. Faith Community: Where You Worship, Learn, and Are Cared For

The faith community is the first and most obvious of the discipleship environments. It's the environment in which we gain our foundation, collectively worship, and are encouraged in the faith. If you grew up in church, you understand the benefits as well as the struggles of the faith community. Church is messy because people are messy. And people always seem to get in the way (other people, of course). The heart and soul of this community has always been to create communion with God through worship, Bible study, and prayer. The benefits are undeniable.

Believer, let me beg you to stay connected to the church. Maybe you need a new form of expression, but don't give up on the bride of Christ. You need her, and she needs you. It seems as though the church is more open today to constructive criticism of how we do what we do with the hopes of honoring and proclaiming Christ and not just defending Christ.

It feels like a new day for the church. Believers are becoming more vulnerable about our shortfalls and are collectively looking for solutions. I like this. Because I believe in the church. Bottom line, we are the church. We'll either be a part of the solution or we'll remain a part of the problem. I hope you'll join or rejoin the fight.

2. Missional Community: Where You Serve and Who You Serve With

I'm a huge fan of the underdog. So is my wife. And my kids. But we weren't always. There was a day when the Hatmaker clan's faith was pretty self-absorbed. It's an embarrassing thought but true. Maybe you have a great faith community around you, but you have no place to serve. Maybe your community is a community of consumers. Or maybe you serve but do it alone. Any of these is bad news.

A missional community is best defined as a smaller group of people gathered around a specific mission or task. The characteristic of a missional community that I believe most profoundly creates an environment of transformation is a commitment to serving the poor, the broken, the marginalized, and the abandoned. The "least of these" (see Matthew 25:40, 45).

I wrote a book on this, called *Barefoot Church: Serving the Least in a Consumer Culture*, and helped start a church focused on missional community. Serving through community has changed the way the Hatmaker family views so many things. It's offered us a new way to see the place possessions hold in our lives, it's revolutionized the way we spend our time, and it has brought a level of depth to our relationships that we never expected. I assure you, this environment is life-altering for everyone involved.

---

3. Secular Community: Where You Really Do Life

The third environment of transformation is close to home. Literally. It's where we spend most of our time when we're not at church. It's our neighborhoods, our workplaces, our schools, and our city centers. For some reason, Christians tend to skip over the opportunities to find community with those closest to us.

The ultimate task of a disciple is to become a missionary to our culture. That means we need to learn to express our faith appropriately in any environment and not keep it compartmentalized. Too often we're either super awkward or unknowingly condescending when we get around people who don't like church, understand church, or do church . . . so this might require a huge shift in thinking for most.

For years the church has encouraged new believers to leave their secular communities and replace them with church community seven days a week. While there are some aspects of secular community where we definitely need to evaluate our involvement, I believe a complete removal from this world (friends, neighbors, coworkers, etc.) is a dire mistake. Instead of removing ourselves from that environment, we should focus our growth on learning how to hold to our faith there. We should consider how those places might become our greatest and most natural mission fields.

I first started thinking differently about my secular community—let's just call them neighbors—on Halloween. After starting a new church, Jen and I moved into a new neighborhood. As we were considering how we were going to engage the holiday, we decided to forgo spending thousands of dollars on a "fall carnival" in the church parking lot. Instead,

Jen and I threw a mini-carnival in our front yard, complete with a couple of bounce houses, a fire pit, and beverages for all.

Here's what we found out: Halloween is the only day of the year that every neighbor you have is going to leave the comfort of his or her home, walk across the street, and knock on your front door. It's an important family day for normal people. Typically, it's the "church folk" who tend to turn the porch light off, jump in the car, and go to more important places.

Something clicked for us on Halloween. We met more neighbors and made more friends that night than any other night of the year. Those relationships have bridged into some very significant and paradigm-shifting moments.

WHERE DO I START?

Ultimately and eventually, all three of these discipleship environments should overlap in one way or another. Learning to live out the gospel in each is critical. Who we are in one environment is who we should be in the other. That's true discipleship, because it's what Jesus did.

"So where do I start?" you ask. I'll answer that question with another: Which environment do you neglect the most? Most of us tend to lean into one of these environments with 90 percent of our minds, bodies, and souls. We then stick our little toes into a second environment, offering a tithe of our energies (if that). And the majority of us will neglect one of these environments completely.

It doesn't make any sense to press deeper into the environment in which we already thrive (or prefer) when we've hit a discipleship ceiling. The answer isn't to do more of what we're already doing. It's quite possible that the things we're neglecting most need some prayerful attention.

> A deeper faith recognizes that our discipleship journey is simply learning how to live as Jesus lived.

A deeper faith recognizes that our discipleship journey is simply learning how to live as Jesus lived in each of these environments. They represent the crossroads between the Great Commission, to make disciples, and the Great Commandment, to love God and love others more deeply, where life meets life, and where every relationship is intentional and every action an opportunity to see his kingdom come, on earth as it is in heaven.

DISCUSSION QUESTIONS

1. In the beginning of the chapter, Brandon discussed how growing up in church shaped and often limited his view of spiritual development. How have your past experiences informed the way you view discipleship?
2. Which of those experiences or influencers would you consider to be positive? Which of them were limiting? How so?
3. How does a holistic view of the gospel shape your view of discipleship? Give an example.
4. Brandon mentioned three different environments where we

learn to be better disciples: (1) the faith community (2) the missional community, and (3) the secular community. Of all the discipleship environments, where do you feel most comfortable? Why?

5. Of all the discipleship environments, which one do you most neglect? Why? How has that impacted your faith?

6. What are some steps you can take to move forward in each of the discipleship environments? How do you anticipate that changing your faith experience?

7. Most of us tend to compartmentalize our discipleship. What other areas of your life remain the most untouched by a deliberate discipleship effort?

8. In this chapter, Brandon discussed Paul's instruction to the Romans to consider the process of Salvation → Presentation → Transformation. If each was a point on a timeline, where would you place yourself at this moment?

9. How does a holistic view of discipleship change the role your small group community, Bible study, or home group plays in your spiritual development?

10. What can this group do to help you on your journey?

CHAPTER 5

A BETTER COMMUNITY

And let us consider how we may spur one another
on toward love and good deeds, not giving up
meeting together, as some are in the habit of
doing, but encouraging one another—and all
the more as you see the Day approaching.

—HEBREWS 10:24-25

I FIRST SAW Crump as he leaned his Harley-Davidson Low Rider onto its kickstand in the parking lot of the Texas Hill Country biker bar. As he entered the front door, fingers combing through his slightly graying beard, his eyes surveyed the room before landing on me. He gave me a familiar nod as he began to work his way to my table.

Crump's dad died when he was just five. He and his younger

sister and brother were raised under the guidance of a mom who struggled with addiction and a stepdad who did his best to stand in the gap. He was a survivor who, in his own words, refused to be a victim of any circumstance. He kept most people at arm's length. You could see it in his walk. Something about it said, "Stay back. You've got a lot to prove before I let you into my head."

Crump was a believer, but wasn't exactly a fan of the church. In fact, the last time he met with a pastor, Crump ended the conversation by inviting him to the parking lot to fight. That was eight years ago. After more than a decade of trying to fit a square peg in a round hole, he decided it was best to just believe in Jesus and skip the church part.

This was the first time I'd ever sat down with Crump one-on-one. Although he knew I was a pastor at the time, we had several friends in common who thought we might get along. That, and a mutual love for motorcycles, seemed to be a good start. I didn't know much about him. But I knew enough to know he was conflicted with the modern church. He was quick to share his view on how self-preservation, public opinion, and personal agenda had ruined church for him. His journey was marked by years of investing into relationships that were eventually discarded for the sake of protecting and defending what he believed to be the wrong things. He felt disposable. The distrust he'd learned as a child was reconfirmed as an adult by the church.

"I've learned a lot about people and community over the years," he said. "And I've learned something about myself: I'm allergic to fake people and fake community. I'm done. Not with Jesus; with his followers. I don't have time for that anymore."

Crump didn't leave much room for small talk. He was a deep thinker who enjoyed raw and honest conversation.

Something clicked with us, and we quickly became friends. At least once a week we would jump on our Harleys for a run through the Hill Country. The pit-stop conversations about life, family, and faith over a greasy hamburger and a local brew were as good as the ride. If not better.

About a month into our friendship, we were grabbing a coffee before an early-morning ride when I told him, "I need to tell you something, and it's important to me that you believe me."

"What's that?" he replied.

"I don't care if you come to my church."

He looked at me with one eyebrow raised.

"I want you to know that's not why I spend time with you. I just enjoy being around you. It's the most honest and refreshing conversation I have each week. My goal isn't to try and get you to come to my church. My goal is to be a good friend."

He just nodded and took a sip of coffee.

It seemed obvious he wasn't going to give me any verbal affirmation at the time, but it was clear he wasn't surprised. He already knew there was something deeper to what was going on. The truth is, I agreed with the majority of his observations. Too often the church under-delivers when it comes to the things that matter. Time after time Crump had heard believers say one thing but live something else. More specifically, he had experienced a lack of love and empathy. Relationships seemed superficial. He hungered for community but didn't trust his Sunday school class or weekly small group. He felt as if he was the only one willing to be honest.

While he valued Bible study and conversation, Crump wasn't a big sermon and Sunday service guy. He didn't enjoy the music. People were the reason he ever went to church, and they were ultimately the reason he left. He yearned for more meaningful relationships, more purposeful tasks, and a more significant legacy than what he was experiencing.

Crump is just one example of the good people struggling in church, considering leaving the church, or who have left the church already. I have seen too many similarly painful experiences in my twenty-plus years of ministry. Some are the fault of those leaving. Some are the fault of those staying. Some are a little of both. Either way there are real emotions in the wake of whatever happened. And it forever changes how people view things.

Most of the people I see struggling with church today aren't frustrated because of what happens on Sunday mornings. Most are frustrated because of what's *not* happening. People are searching for connection on a deeper level. Maybe you can relate. You've got friends you tend to gravitate to in the hallways. You've got people who will grab a coffee with you if you ask. But you're starving for that deep connection with others you can literally do life and faith with. You're missing people in your life who can tell there's something wrong just by seeing the look on your face or by hearing the tone in your voice. You're hungry for true community. Biblical community. The kind we read about happening in the early church and the kind we saw with Jesus and his disciples.

Today, Crump comes to our church . . . sometimes. Mostly on days he volunteers to help set up. When he doesn't come, it doesn't bother me because I don't think the way we do church matches the way Crump does church. He comes to see his friends. And he comes for his wife and his daughter. He grows through conversation, not through sermons. In his words, "All life is discipleship."

I've always been relationally drawn to those on the margins, and I've come to realize that I'm never going to have a place in a guy like Crump's life by inviting him to a Sunday church service, no matter how creative and insightful the next great message series is. To him, the idea of church leadership comes with a gag reflex that triggers all kinds of negative emotions. Instead, I've learned to listen in order to gain a fresh perspective into the experiences and pain of people like him. I've learned to love differently, and it has directly impacted nearly every relationship I have for the good.

As a part of the church, I truly believe this is how we should respond with the love of God. Until we do so, we'll never hear the question behind the question or the need behind the need. Instead, we'll find ourselves in a holy huddle, surrounded only by people who think like us and act like us.

The lessons I'm learning with Crump aren't so much about learning a new way to do church. They're about developing a new way to do community, starting with real friendships, not just conveniently hanging out with another random couple from church who happens to live in my subdivision.

Today, I get together with Crump and about a dozen other bikers once a month. Although maybe only half the guys are believers, they still call it "church." We meet in the back room of a bar to plan our next ride, decide on our next service project, and vote on what community benefits we want to support. About four years ago we formalized our group into an official motor-cycle club and are a part of the United Clubs of Austin. Together we partner with foster families and work with abused children to help with needs they might have. In addition to our monthly "church," we get together once a month with all our spouses and have family night. Nearly every time we meet up, we end up riding somewhere and usually stop at some dive bar, which always leads to more great conversations about life, family, and faith.

There's a special kind of community with these men that I've rarely seen on the church campus. It's pretty raw. And outside of pretending we're a little tougher than we really are, everyone has permission to be himself. There's nothing that could be said that would surprise anyone at the table—although it takes a while to get used to hearing cussing in one sentence followed by, "Let's pray" in the next (we close every meeting with a short devotional and prayer). It's sometimes dirty, but it's always beautiful.

It's a surprising mixture of all three discipleship environments we discussed in the last chapter—secular community, missional community, and faith community. That's what I think is so refreshing about what I'm experiencing with my motorcycle club. It started in a secular environment, transitioned into a form of mission once we added service projects that took the focus off ourselves, and for some is now becoming a unique type of faith community, all outside of a traditional church environment. It truly has the potential to become gospel community. But it won't just happen automatically; it requires intentionality and happens best in the context of genuine relationships.

Some of the most meaningful groups I've experienced started

organically with friendships and moved toward a form of discipleship or Bible study. Traditional church groups tend to start with discipleship or Bible study and end with the same . . . more discipleship and more Bible study. To be clear, I'm not saying that it's impossible to experience gospel community through a traditional Bible study or similar group. I've seen it happen plenty of times. What I'm saying is that it rarely happens without intentionally digging into the real lives of those involved.

Jesus always seemed to create a redemptive environment of belonging that led people toward believing and becoming, no matter where he was and what he was doing. This trajectory was primary to his life and teaching, and they continue to be our guide for not just a better community, but for the best community imaginable. It's his dream for us.

A NEW WAY TO BELONG

We don't have members at my church. Instead, we have partners. While the label pretty much means the same thing as what we might traditionally think, we're intentional about the name change because it also comes with a bit of a paradigm shift.

When I hear the word *member*, it makes me think about joining a country club. Membership comes with privileges and rights, because you paid for them and the club exists to serve you. You're either in or you're out. It's the same at Sam's Club or Costco. If you're not a member, you're not welcome; if you are a member, you get special discounts for stuff you need (and want).

You might *belong* in that place, but it's not because of who you are. It's because of what you've done. You paid your dues, and now you're entitled.

I've never had a membership at a country club, but I've had friends who do. The first time I visited a country club as a guest, I felt incredibly uncomfortable. While no one really knew who I was, I felt as though everyone knew I didn't belong. My friend was running late, and I kept waiting for someone to ask me who I was and why I was there. Although my friend was the president of a local bank and a lifetime member of the club, I feared I was going to be escorted off the property if caught before he got there.

Partners, on the other hand, make me think of a law firm. If you are a partner, you have a personal interest in the company. It's more personal than having a membership and is more about who you are. You're vested. And if the company goes down, you go down. When you are a partner, you don't work *for* the company; in many ways you *are* the company. At the partner level you have agreed upon a certain direction for the organization, and everyone is in it together. You've considered the costs, the risks, and the rewards in advance.

Partners have ownership. They get a key to the building and the code to the alarm system. They get access at all times, because they *belong* at all times. Loyalty to the success of the organization and the mission is prioritized over personal agendas because as partners, whatever is best for the company is best for us. To become a partner requires a shift in thinking and a shift in priorities.

As believers, we can't just sign up and pay our dues for gospel community. We can't simply attend, skeptically waiting to see if the group is going to meet our needs, with one finger on the ejector seat button. We need to take ownership, to see ourselves *belonging* in community. It should be a place where our unbelieving friends can see themselves belonging as well. It should be a space that energizes and refreshes us, an environment where we not only feel accepted; we are accepted, and because of that, the table is set for true spiritual depth and searching. In true gospel community, we can be honest about personal struggles and professional mishaps. We might even get a little glimpse of the kingdom right in the middle of our living rooms or around our tables on a normal Wednesday night.

There are a handful of factors that lead to this kind of community, namely *vulnerability, permission,* and *inclusivity.* Let's look at each:

Vulnerability

Over the past twenty years, the church in America has gone through many phases of leadership styles and growth strategies. We've moved from seeker-sensitive to purpose-driven to culturally relevant to postmodern (and beyond). During this time, the word *authentic* has been used to describe numerous programs, studies, and sermon series. What that typically meant was the event you were about to attend or message you were about to hear would be authentic to our culture. It would make sense in context, and would be something that we could apply to our everyday life. As I look back now, that's not really the definition of *authentic* that I was hoping for. I was hoping for a raw and honest look behind the curtain. I wanted transparency. Somewhere deep inside I realized that the cost of true authenticity was vulnerability. That's what my soul craved: vulnerability.

True gospel community starts with true vulnerability. It's where *we* end and the gospel begins. It's a space of confession where we invite others into our lives to care for us, speak truth to us, empathize with us, and help us find forgiveness. It's the place where servant leaders lead. For some reason vulnerability resists judgment, and it fosters grace and understanding. There's nothing more refreshing than seeing friends handle your most vulnerable moments with care or a leader trusting you with his or hers. It's the place we are healed.

> True gospel community starts with true vulnerability. It's where *we* end and the gospel begins.

Paul taught a lot about community in his letter to Rome. And of all the ways he could choose to begin the conversation, here's how he started:

> For by the grace given me I say to every one of you: Do not think of yourself more highly than you ought, but rather think of yourself with sober judgment, in accordance with the faith God has distributed to each of you. (Romans 12:3)

Vulnerability requires personal humility. This is why we struggle so much. Pride gets involved and overrides our willingness to be vulnerable. Left undiagnosed, we have no chance at community. It requires looking inward first.

Permission

Permission starts with us. First and foremost, we have to give ourselves permission to be vulnerable before anyone else will. It starts with being honest about everything related to the group (with some discernment utilized). This is easier said than done. I've seen people, for the sake of unity, keep their opinions and desires to themselves, allowing bitterness to grow and destroying what they were trying to protect in the first place. This is anything but redemptive. I've seen this happen because of something as big as a theological disagreement to something as seemingly insignificant as a misplaced e-mail.

From there we have to extend the same permission to others. We can't keep it for ourselves. It's impossible to move forward, much less go deeper, if we can't find a common ground in this area. This standard will create a healthier group dynamic, producing space for non-agenda-driven and honest conversations. Questions can be asked without judgment, and we'll instantly experience a new level of freedom and connectivity.

Bottom line, permission fosters trust. Trust triggers the environment for a redemptive response. I believe with all my heart that most people want this, and it is a necessary part of true community. As Stephen Covey put it, "Trust is the glue of life. It's the most essential ingredient in effective communication. It's the foundational principle that holds all relationships."[1]

Inclusivity

As a church leader, I try to visit another church at least a couple of times a year to remind myself what it feels like to be an outsider. Here's what I've concluded: church can be weird.

Maybe not for you, but for someone who didn't grow up in church, it's weird. Think about it for a moment. First, you have to work your way through the greeter gauntlet at the door. Then you enter a crowded room where most everyone avoids eye contact. You make your way to the visitor booth, and someone asks you to wear a name tag that lets everyone know you are visiting. (Also, can you give us your phone number and e-mail address, so we can stalk you when you leave? Thanks.) Once you find a seat, the band starts playing songs you've never heard. Everyone stands to sing, some clapping, some raising their hands, and some crying. They hand you a book over two thousand pages long and tell you to turn to Amos. Then the pastor starts talking about the Pharisees, the Sadducees, the Philistines, and the Maccabees. They want you to understand Jesus' propitiation and plan for reconciliation so you can have justification, redemption, and salvation. At the end, they ask you to give 10 percent of your paycheck to some guy standing in the aisle, holding a velvet bag with a brass ring around it.

Some of these things are a necessary part of doing Sunday church. All of them come with good intentions. And while I'm intentionally overstating the experience, most of these things work against making those not familiar with church culture feel welcome.

It's nearly impossible to do Sunday church without using insider language and making nonbelievers feel like outsiders. There's such a huge cultural gap between the believing world and the secular world. It's incredibly difficult to completely close that gap without compromising the message and the purposes of corporate worship.

Maybe that's why Jesus seemed to start at a different place. He started by creating a common ground.

To follow his example, we must see that it can be more effective to invite someone into our homes than it is to invite him or her to church. There's no better place for a friend or neighbor to first experience the gospel than in our living rooms or at our dinner tables. We should go to great lengths making sure we've created a judgment-free zone. This includes ensuring that the other believers you invite into that space are on the same page with you. This might become a real challenge when it comes to varying theological views and political beliefs, but we have to make sure our Christian friends can be trusted with our non-believing friends. This means they have to receive newcomers as they are, trusting that God is big enough to move them forward and knowing that our job is to love them, accept them, and represent the gospel well. Then we may actually earn a place in their lives to be trusted with input about their eternity.

As disciples we need to learn this together. We need to give ourselves permission to slow down and think beyond this coming Sunday. But one thing's for sure: when you have true gospel community, nearly anyone can walk into the room and feel welcome. This is just one way our lives become worship. As the apostle Paul put it in his letter to Rome, "Accept one another, then, just as Christ accepted you, in order to bring praise to God" (Romans 15:7).

Here's the bonus truth: while I believe it's important to invite people into your lives without agenda, once true friendships are made, others are much more likely to be curious about your church life. Not everyone will make the jump, but you'll see much more traction in the context of genuine relationships than you will any other way.

OWNING IT

Not long ago I was invited to coffee by a church attender who had been around for about six months. Before coming to our church, he and his wife were longtime members of a different church in town and actually led the home group ministry there for several years. We exchanged pleasantries for a few minutes before he let me know the reason for our meeting. They had decided to leave our church. In his own words, they couldn't get "connected."

As soon as I heard his words, I remembered seeing him come early to the church with his wife on Sundays and find their seats among the empty chairs while everyone else was hanging out and visiting in the lobby. The vast majority of the people at church were getting to know each other, talking, and laughing, while they were staring at an empty stage.

I remembered an e-mail from them requesting help getting connected, followed by my reply offering them three options: a partner class, a men's get-together, and a missional community that met in their neighborhood. They didn't attend any of them.

Community in itself is hard work, much less biblical community. It requires digging. It requires sacrifice. It requires some uncomfortable moments, but more than anything it requires just showing up. No one can connect us better than we can connect ourselves. And our church staff can't make us do anything we don't really want to do.

To be honest, for nearly every moment when I've felt on the outside, there was a decision along the way where I chose something else instead of community. Whether it was just wanting to stay home a certain night because I was tired, or not preparing well for a discussion or forgetting a food item I was supposed to bring, or failing to respond to an RSVP as the leader asked, there was always some way to stay out of the game. We all tend to drop the ball if we're not thinking intentionally.

BREAKING THE NORM

I have a confession to make. I'm highly opinionated about this topic, because I don't fit into typical church community. I've rarely enjoyed being funneled into a group made up of people who filled out a card on Sunday morning and happened to live within a five-mile radius of my house. I can do a Bible study or small group with anyone, but I don't intuitively connect with everyone in the room just because we're all Christians. Jen's the same way.

Because of this, we've had to reevaluate how we spend our relational equity and how we pursue community. This typically results in us saying "no" more often. Saying no starts with choosing the right "yes."

There are three kinds of yes that Jen and I have chosen when it comes to community. All three are a little different from the normal church small group. In fact, two of the three groups involve people who don't go to our church or don't go to church at all. The first group is my motorcycle community discussed at the beginning of this chapter. The second is a group that we simply call "supper club."

Supper club started as a dinner with four couples. All have served in some type of church or nonprofit leadership, and all have large families. Three of the four couples have adopted internationally, and all of us like good food. None of us go to the same church, yet we instantly have affinity in three major areas of life: faith, family, and food.

We meet once a month and rotate houses each month. No kids are allowed. Whoever is hosting is in charge of everything, from food to cleanup. So only once a quarter is one couple hosting and doing all the work; the other three months we get to just show up and enjoy.

Each time we meet, we have a discussion question. Topics vary from serious, such as "Share your best and worst parenting moment of the year," to ridiculous discussions like "Would you rather be rich or famous?" We glide seamlessly from moments of hilarity to tears and back to hilarity nearly every time we get together. It's incredibly honest, and nothing is off-limits. Although we don't do Bible study at supper club, I would consider every gathering incredibly spiritual, encouraging, and redemptive.

Supper club has morphed from a monthly dinner to occasional Friday playdates to even a few summer vacations together. Since we have such big families, there's always a friend for each kid to play with. All the guys like each other, and the girls could talk all night (literally). There's something special about supper club. We could go a whole month without seeing each other, yet somehow when we get together we never skip a beat. It's become a judgment-free zone where we all just enjoy each other's company. It's also drama-free. And it's one of our favorite nights of the month.

Our third group we call SNC, which stands for Sunday Night Church.

SNC started several years ago when we first helped plant Austin New Church (ANC). Each Sunday evening, we would get together with two of our closest friend couples after the kids would go to bed. Since there's an occasional cigar along with a glass of wine, we always meet outside on one of our patios. It's amazing what a couple of misting fans can do in the summer and an overhead propane heater can do in the winter to make the evening just perfect in Texas.

Everyone involved with SNC goes to Austin New Church, volunteers, or serves in leadership in one form or another. We each live and breathe ANC, so for the most part we talk shop about church that day. It's a debriefing of sorts. We each share what we thought was good about the Sunday service and what needed improvement. Since we are a church plant, we often joke about fearing the inevitable Sunday when no one shows up. Fortunately, after eight years, someone always does.

From there we check in with each other on how everyone is doing. We talk about our kids, our marriages, and our struggles. We've lived through everything from middle school drama to helping choose college dorms and meal plans. SNC is a sacred place where we can vent our frustrations and encourage one another. We've cried, laughed, prayed, cussed at, and made fun of each other. We've survived high school graduations together and mourned deaths in the family together. Each Sunday night there's a patio just south of Austin, Texas, that turns into a sanctuary of sorts, and it's life-giving.

Of all the groups, each one holds a special place in our hearts. Each seems to play a different role and scratch a certain "itch," if you will. I'd sink without them. I wouldn't trade them for the world.

That said, there is one thing all these groups have in common that is the deciding factor in getting a "yes" from the Hatmakers: they are enjoyable.

Maybe that sounds overly simple, but it's true. I've had groups that were a drag, and every time I went, I felt as if I died a little inside. I've been in groups that have just worn me plumb out, and I'd come home exhausted. I would dread going to them, so now I don't go anymore. Instead, I go to supper club. I go to SNC. And I go to "church" with my biker brothers. I look forward to them, every time. Each one has a redemptive quality. All of them energize us and refresh us, because they suit us.

I'll admit, though: finding that kind of community can prove difficult. Although we've always had great friends in our lives, it wasn't until we were in our late thirties and early forties that Jen and I finally found our "community" groove. And it didn't happen until we changed our expectations. We were always hoping for that perfect Bible study, that perfect teacher, or for that perfect church.

The problem is that the church is filled with people just like you and me, broken people who are still *becoming*. People who are striving to know and be known by God and others. People still clambering for the top of the ladder, hoping they're doing it for the right reasons and that somehow they're on the right ladder. Sometimes we've got to fight ourselves and think outside the box to pursue community, but in the end community is worth fighting for.

REASONS WE MISS COMMUNITY

My dad always taught me that you can't control what other people do; you can only control what you do and how you respond to other people. The longer I live, the more that proves true.

So instead of starting with "what's wrong with everyone else?" (wink, wink), let's do a little self-evaluating to see where we might be getting in the way of us finding what we're looking for. Here are a few questions to ask ourselves:

Do I have realistic expectations? Often, we tend to expect from our peers what we're not willing or able to give ourselves. If we are constantly disappointed or frustrated with others' levels of commitment or investment, forgetting that they have real life going on as well, we will miss community. It's hard for others to see or meet our needs when they're dealing with family problems, marriage struggles, and work issues. Are *you* being the friend you want to have? If we're honest, most of us want someone to prove his or her friendship or commitment to community before we're willing to reciprocate. But it's a process to get there, and someone has to go first.

A second place we typically have unrealistic expectations regarding community is with our pastors. This one is personal for me, because I have served in church leadership for so long. The truth is that most congregants expect too much from their pastors relationally. Even with the best intentions, it's impossible for a pastor to be best friends with and know what's going on with everyone in a congregation at all times, even with Facebook. I struggled for years with shame and feeling I could never do enough. It was a milestone in my own emotional health as a leader once I accepted the fact that I can't be everything for everyone.

Some of you may be best friends with your pastor or church leaders, but most of us need to find our key spiritual relationships with others just like us. The journey together is what community is all about. We get to learn together as we grow together. I promise you, you'll probably have way more fun with your pastor not in the room. Maybe you can be yourself with him there . . . but most of your friends and neighbors can't.

Am I being vulnerable? Let's be real with ourselves. Are we being honest in our group? This struggle can take many forms. A leader of a group may struggle with this more than anyone. There is a real pressure to feeling that you have to have all the answers and be worthy of being followed. This pressure keeps us from sharing honestly about things we don't do well or even struggle to believe theologically.

Other individuals in the group may struggle with vulnerability because they struggle with trusting the group. So let's go there. Are you trustworthy? Does what's said in the group stay in the group, or does it somehow become fodder for gossip outside the community? If so, you need to put a stop to it, or it will be like cancer to community.

Maybe you talk too much. Oops. I said it. Sorry. But every group I've been a part of has that person who dominates conversation. *All. The. Time.* Is it you? If so, why? Usually that person thinks it's because he or she has all the answers and just really needs to share them. But what I've also found to be true is that people who talk all the time usually feel as if they have something to prove, are hiding something, or at minimum, are deflecting. I'm not accusing here, just trying to help your group be more vulnerable. Soak it up for a moment.

Regardless of the reason, if you feel that your group has remained in the shallows and vulnerability is the reason, take a moment to discuss why that might be. Start with asking questions, not giving answers. Maybe start by simply asking, "What's keeping us from being more vulnerable with each other?" and "What can we do to be more vulnerable?"

Am I in the wrong group? This one may hurt a little. And might be the most difficult to deal with. But if you just don't look forward to the group, it's not going to last long anyway. If you've applied or addressed all the other issues we've discussed but nothing seems to change, then maybe you're just a passenger on the wrong bus. Or, if you're the leader, maybe you're trying to drive the wrong bus.

Not all groups are for everyone. Different people value the place of Bible study in community, the place of fellowship in community, and even the place of kids in community. Maybe you need an adults-only group, but half of your group values doing community with their families. My recommendation is to stop trying to change each other's preferences and find or start a group that's on the same page or in the same stage of life. These aren't issues of right and wrong and shouldn't be relational deal breakers. They should just be discussed as realities. Embrace change as a part of the journey. Remember: no drama.

Do I feel disconnected? We can feel disconnected for a number of reasons. Some are because of the issues we've already discussed, but some are just because we *are* disconnected.

Here's the truth: if it's been a month since you've attended a weekly group, it's likely you'll start feeling uninformed. If you attend one or two times out of four, you'll probably start feeling out of the loop. It's possible, then, that there's nothing wrong with the community at all; rather, something is off with you. It's important for each of us to evaluate this so we don't cast blame, get bitter, and withdraw even more.

Stage of life can have a lot to do with it. Maybe your family is in an extremely busy season with youth sports, maybe you're in month three of a newborn in the house, or maybe work has you on the ropes. If either is the case, adding a Bible study or small group can become quite a chore.

I would recommend trying one of three things in this situation:

1. **Say no to something else.** Take a hard look at your weekly calendar, and evaluate how you spend your time. You might even take the time to rate all your regularly scheduled events according to how necessary or important they are. To free up more time, maybe you can find something else you can say no to in order to say yes to your community group.

2. **Invest more deeply in current relationships.** Sometimes we add a church group to our schedules and end up pulling ourselves out of our most natural mission field. Perhaps instead we just need to figure out how to invest more deeply in an existing group of friends that aligns more naturally with our current schedule. Maybe it's a playgroup with other moms of newborns. Or maybe you could add in social time with coworkers, or invest more deeply in the other parents of your kid's sports teams. Everyone gets some of you; no one gets all of you. Whatever it is, be intentional, and schedule something regular. You'd be amazed how those friendships can turn into fulfilling and even meaningful community.

3. **Take a break.** If neither of these work, maybe you just need to take a break from the group for a season. It's okay. You're allowed to call time-out. There really are busier seasons of life that will pass if you can endure them. No one knows if this is healthy for you other than you. Be prayerful about it, and pursue it as a type of fast or sabbatical. And if you do this, it's key that you make a commitment and choose a time in advance to start back. Include your existing community in this decision by asking for their prayer, asking permission to drop in maybe once a month or so to check back in, and integrate a little accountability by letting them know when you're coming back. This is a tough one and can easily be a permanent exit if you're not cautious. Doing it right is key.

A DEEPER COMMUNITY

Some of you reading this already have amazing biblical community. You study God's Word together, you pray together, and you
are vulnerable together. Maybe you would say absolutely everything is going great, but you might admit that you could use a
little fresh wind in your sails every now and then. Or maybe
your group seems to be doing great, but you're having a hard
time inviting friends and neighbors. This is common with a
tight group, because visitors often feel like outsiders. With this
in mind, here are a few suggestions you can try to deepen what
you already have or to invite friends to join you in a different
environment:

1. **Add mission.** We've seen some life instantly breathed into
   a group by taking one meeting out of the month and
   replacing the typical Bible study with a service project
   in that neighborhood or city. This not only breaks up the
   routine but helps point a group outward that is typically
   focused inward. It's amazing how a neighbor will jump
   in for a service project. Serving together provides a great
   environment to get to know someone new.
2. **Inject some fun.** Maybe your group is awesome, but you
   just need to get together on a more social level. If so,
   make it happen! Start a monthly get-together focused
   on relationships. Start a rotation of dinner dates with
   couples in the group. Add a poker night for the fellas, a
   book club for the ladies, a movie night, a monthly concert
   downtown, or a day at the lake with a few of the families.

Whatever it is, get out and have fun together at least once a quarter.

3. **Make it more interactive.** Anything you do to change the schedule once a month can be helpful. Maybe, instead of a Bible study, make the first meeting of the month more discussion oriented or do a personal checkup with everyone in the group to see how they are doing. We add what we call "high/low" to our group at least once each month by asking each participant to share his or her best and worst moments of the month. It doesn't have to be hyper-spiritual; just encourage sharing about what's going on in real life. This can be a great way to get a prayer list going as well.

4. **Diversify your schedule.** Even the best of things can become rote if you do the same thing week after week. One way to diversify a Bible study or home group is to meet for your traditional group the first and third weeks and then do something more social on the second and fourth weeks. Our church encourages taking one of the "off weeks" to do something neighborhood-focused on the second weeks and something mission-focused on the fourth weeks (see suggestion #1). What ends up happening is everyone goes to dinner after the service projects, and we foster community within our group, including our families, and doing some good along the way.

5. **Celebrate family dynamics.** Every family-aged group struggles with what to do with the kids. Sometimes it ends up dividing a group, because some want their whole family involved while others just need a break from the

kiddos. While I would suggest having some groups that include kids and some groups that don't, that's not always possible or ideal. One of the ways you can address this need or desire is to adopt the meeting rhythm discussed in suggestion #3, which can allow you to include the kids on the neighborhood and mission weeks. For the remaining Bible study weeks, we recommend focusing one weekly gathering on just adults—turn it into a date night of sorts, and get a babysitter once a month—and one week on a family study including the kids. Sometimes that family study can involve a project for the kids, prepping for the service or mission project the next week. I honestly think this might be the most reasonable, considerate, and realistic of all the schedules if you want a truly holistic group.

6. **Add break-out groups.** Groups can deepen their intimacy simply by spending the last fifteen to thirty minutes breaking out into guys and gals for a prayer time or closing discussion. Both men and women seem to be more vulnerable in gender-specific settings. You don't have to do it every week. In fact, if the reason you're doing this is to add some change or freshen up your group, I'd recommend you only do it once a month or so. This will make that one gathering different from all the others.

7. **Increase your hang time.** This might be the most difficult because of time constraints but can be incredibly productive. Whether you do it every week or once a month,

consider adding a meal, a coffee time, or simply desserts to your gathering. Whatever it is, be sure to schedule in an extra hour or so before or after your meeting with some unstructured hang time, and make it optional. This will keep people from checking their watches, and natural conversation will ensue. There's something special that happens around a dinner table that doesn't seem to happen anywhere else.

A shallow religion survives from event to event and program to program. A deeper faith is rooted in trusting relationships where permission is granted to struggle, fail, and take risks. It's a place where questions are welcomed and everyone is a learner again. Where the scabs of loneliness, emptiness, and false hope are ripped off and replaced with a concern for others, a place to be propped up, and a shared gospel worth living for.

> A shallow religion survives from event to event and program to program. A deeper faith is rooted in trusting relationships where permission is granted to struggle, fail, and take risks.

Whatever you do, do something. Community is one of the most significant elements of a growing faith, yet it's one of the most neglected. We'll fill our weekly schedule with church campus activities but struggle to find a single day to focus on deepening our relationships. Please don't lose sight of community. I'm convinced it's worth the effort.

DISCUSSION QUESTIONS

1. Have you ever found community in an unlikely place or with an unexpected group of people? What do you think created that sense of community? What can we learn from your experience?

2. Have you ever thought about your small group or community group as a biblical or "gospel community" where the gospel can work in you and through you for the sake of others? How is this similar to or different from how you've traditionally viewed church small groups?

3. On a scale of 1 to 10 how would you rate yourself on being vulnerable? Why is that?

4. How do you think giving permission to be more vulnerable and honest can lead to more trust? What impact should that have on your spiritual growth? Why?

5. What is the entry point for your group for a new person? Would a visitor instantly feel welcome? Why or why not? What can or should you do to change that?

6. One thing about embracing diversity is that not everyone finds community in the same way. Do you most naturally find a sense of community in or outside a traditional church environment? Why do you think that is?

7. Toward the end of the chapter, we discussed reasons we typically miss out on community. Do you identify with one of the reasons more than the others? If so, which one?

8. Have you ever felt disconnected from a group or church? What happened? What did you learn from the experience?

9. Have you ever had a stage in life where you had to just take a time-out from any small groups or community groups at church? What did you learn from that time? Benefits? Struggles?

10. We discussed seven ways you can deepen existing community. Which one resonates most with you? Why?

PART II

THE GOSPEL THROUGH US

CHAPTER 6

A CLOSER KINGDOM

"I will give you the keys of the kingdom of heaven."

−MATTHEW 16:19

JEN AND I have five kids. All five are amazing. Three of them, as Jen likes to say, we had the old-fashioned way. The youngest two we adopted. Ben and Remy are bright and inquisitive, have huge hearts for other people, and have been a joy to watch as they adjust to life in the Hatmaker family.

Since they both came from Ethiopia, you can probably imagine the culture shock. New things, new fascinations, and new priorities were everywhere. One of the most memorable was related to what some claim to be the center of the American home: the television. While Ben and Remy had exposure to movies and cartoon videos in the orphanage, TV in all its glory was fairly new to them.

At the beginning we were super selective as to what we let them watch. Parenting controls made Netflix a safe home base. After several months of controlled viewing, we introduced them to the world of network TV. Ben quickly found what would become his nemesis: commercials. For him, they always seemed to come at the most unwelcome times, and he simply could not grasp why anyone would put a completely unrelated ad in the middle of his show.

He was so frustrated that we had to prepare him in advance when we knew commercials were coming. He would just sit there with arms crossed, trying not to get angry, but we could see him stewing (the dramatic sighing made his frustration pretty obvious). He's since sworn off network TV at least a dozen times.

Remy, on the other hand, had different kinds of issues with the TV. She was fascinated with what she saw, but it blew her mind a bit. She couldn't quite reconcile real life and TV reality. She didn't have anger issues, but she certainly had questions:

Remy: Is Jessie real?

Jen: She is just a character on TV.

Remy: Oh, she's a cartoon?

Jen: No, a real person is playing Jessie.

Remy: Where is the real Jessie?

Jen: There is no real Jessie.

Remy: Oh, she's dead?

Jen: No! Jessie is a made-up person.

Remy: She's a drawing?

Jen: Remy. A human actress plays a fake character named Jessie.

Remy: But where does Jessie live?

Jen: Jessie doesn't exist in the real world.

Remy: Oh! She lives in heaven?

Jen: Yes. Fine. Okay. Jessie is a cartoon drawing who lives in heaven.

She just couldn't get it. She could not figure out how to reconcile these two worlds.

Jesus spent most of his earthly ministry trying to help the disciples reconcile two worlds: the kingdom they lived in and understood, and the kingdom of God. In every possible way Jesus kept trying to explain to his followers that things, according to the wisdom of God, are different from what we expect them to be. God's kingdom doesn't look one iota like earthly power structures, and God doesn't look one iota like earthly rulers.

KINGDOM IDENTITY

In the Sermon on the Mount, Jesus spoke of the kingdom of heaven and completely redefined what it looked like to be a disciple through a section we've come to know as the Beatitudes:

> Blessed are the poor in spirit,
> > for theirs is the kingdom of heaven.
> Blessed are those who mourn,
> > for they will be comforted.

Blessed are the meek,
>   for they will inherit the earth.
Blessed are those who hunger and thirst for righteousness,
>   for they will be filled.
Blessed are the merciful,
>   for they will be shown mercy.
Blessed are the pure in heart,
>   for they will see God.
Blessed are the peacemakers,
>   for they will be called children of God.
Blessed are those who are persecuted because of
>   righteousness,
>   for theirs is the kingdom of heaven. (Matthew 5:3–10)

The reality of the kingdom is found at both the beginning and the end of the Beatitudes. Starting with the poor in spirit and ending with those who suffer for the sake of righteousness, Jesus declared, "for theirs is the kingdom of heaven." Between these two kingdom bookends we find the characteristics of mournfulness, meekness, righteousness, mercy, purity, and peacemaking.

In a world of power-hungry and corrupt political and military leaders, these pursuits were the exact opposite of what Roman culture valued. It was an audacious departure in what would become known as the most famous sermon in the history of the world.

But the disciples didn't get it. They couldn't reconcile real life with the kingdom Jesus was lifting up.

Jesus continued to spend long hours teaching, and days and nights, weeks and months feeding the hungry and healing people whom the rest of the world had abandoned. He sent his disciples out, not as conquerors but as humble teachers, taking almost nothing with them except the gospel.

He told them that, for the sake of God's kingdom, he was going to have to give up his life, and that anyone who wanted to follow him had to be ready to take up a cross and lose his life as well. And as Jesus taught on giving everything up, what did the disciples do? They argued among themselves about which of them would be the greatest in the kingdom.

They, like most, despite all the teaching and modeling Jesus had done already, still regarded the kingdom as secular, a top-down power system where the greatest was . . . the obvious greatest, wealthiest, most powerful, and those holding the strongest credentials, the most political sway, and the most authority. This was their disconnect.

Jesus is not of this world. His authority is not defined by earthly politics and is not bound by the laws of nature. His office is not up for reelection. His rule is perfect, in need of no counsel, and is forever. Thus, there is no need for a hierarchy of people in his kingdom; there is only need for kingdom people with moral authority to live out the convictions, hopes, and dreams of the king.

Jesus was calling his disciples to exchange all they had known for all he knew. He was calling them to exchange a religion that was sustained with earthly wisdom and position for a faith that was sustained by grace and truth.

But the disciples still found their identity in their accomplishments and assignments instead of in Jesus himself. So in the absence of understanding, they defaulted to the path of greatness they knew.

Surely each one of them had an argument for position in this new kind of kingdom. Or so they thought. And this is exactly where Jesus found them when the disciples asked him, "Who, then, is greatest in the kingdom of heaven?" (Matthew 18:1).

What were they thinking? Well . . .

- Peter was probably the best leader of all the disciples.
- Judas was really good with money.
- Jude typically had the inside scoop, since he was related to Jesus.
- John always seemed to speak Jesus' love language.
- Andrew was the first to actually leave everything behind.

Surely these things counted for something!

This is where most of us get stuck. We find our identity in the spiritual task instead of the spiritual head. We find our confidence and our position in the hope that what we have accomplished or what we have become is enough to earn our place. This, in itself, flies in the face of what Jesus is doing. Our idea of kingdom requires spiritual tasks; Jesus' kingdom requires spiritual surrender. Our place in the kingdom is given to us because Jesus took our place on the cross.

> Our idea of kingdom requires spiritual tasks; Jesus' kingdom requires spiritual surrender.

Instead of rightly asking how they might have the strength and grace to suffer with Jesus, the disciples asked how they might be positioned to reign with him. They wanted the crown, not the cross.

They were still asking, "How can we be bigger?"

Their idea of kingdom was being wrecked by an unsettled identity. The lesson was difficult, because the world sees no greatness in lowliness. So what did Jesus do?

He called a little child to him and placed the child among them (Matthew 18:2).

A toddler has no rank in the political world, no power in society. In a child we see true humility, not manufactured, not insincere, not as a means to an end. It's as if Jesus was saying, "Here is the one excellence on which my kingdom is founded, and by which alone it can be extended—the excellence of not knowing you have any excellence at all."[1]

> And he said: "Truly I tell you, unless you change and become like little children, you will never enter the kingdom of heaven. Therefore, whoever takes the lowly position of this child is the greatest in the kingdom of heaven. And whoever welcomes one such child in my name welcomes me." (Matthew 18:3–5)

Jesus clearly declared that a change must occur. There is a necessary conversion that, if we were to be honest, we are incapable of doing. A grown man cannot become a child. We cannot convert ourselves into this type of humility. Only God can give us a new heart. It's God who transforms. Our part is simply to submit to the process of the gospel making us new again. Matthew Henry put it this way: "Besides the first conversion of a soul from a state of nature to a state of grace, there are after-conversions from particular paths . . . which are equally necessary to salvation."[2]

Every move toward humility is a conversion. Killing pride involves a thousand daily deaths that are hard and hurt and will cost us something. But every time we choose to reject the lie of *bigger* and instead choose little, we are more converted to the greatness of the kingdom.

As we walk through our daily lives, we need to ask ourselves, "How can I be little in this? How can I resist the impulse to be big? Where am I working toward big because I'm afraid of being little in that space or relationship?"

Some of you especially struggle with this because you find yourself in a big space. Maybe you're in a position of power or influence. Maybe you earned your place. Maybe you were given your position. Either way, you find yourself conflicted in your big space. But even then, we need to be continually asking ourselves, "How can I be small even in this big space? How do I steward influence well in my big space? How do I decrease so that Christ might increase? How do I step aside and let Christ reign in this moment?"

Only then will we be truly walking according to God's kingdom.

KINGDOM NOW

When I became a Christian as a young child, all the instruction I remember receiving about the kingdom was to protect myself from the corruption of the world, to avoid spending too much time with "sinners," and to hold on until Jesus came back. I grew up learning more about hoping to be in heaven one day, a kingdom *not yet,* than living a life that chooses the ways of Christ today, a kingdom *now.* Christianity was presented to me more as a waiting game than it was something I could thrive in. Getting to heaven simply meant avoiding hell.

Yet somewhere, deep down, I knew there should be more to life as a Christian than signing up for an eternal fire insurance policy. And there is. In fact, I think it's those who live as though today has no eternal significance who are most confused, empty, and frustrated with their faith.

The fullness of the kingdom goes beyond a one-day-yet-to-come dream; it's also a glimpse into what God has in mind for today. It's a kingdom yet to arrive, but also a kingdom now. Today, we find ourselves in an age of grace beyond the cross but before Christ's second return. How we choose to live in this in-between says a lot about what we believe regarding the kingdom.

Today matters. Your life, your successes, your pain, and your growth this side of eternity are not in vain. When Jesus said, "It is finished" on the cross, he meant it (John 19:30). All that was necessary to usher in the kingdom has already taken place. Now we must respond. We must be ready to live out this reality "on earth as it is in heaven" (see Matthew 6:10).

We are invited into this amazing story of redemption. And it's a story filled with everything else besides waiting.

Here are a few things I've learned—and continue to learn— along the way to help us get past our preconceived ideas and comprehend a closer kingdom, one that is within reach, and the one Jesus said is at hand today:

The kingdom is more of a moment breaking through than a ladder to be climbed. I used to view spiritual growth as a ladder of sorts. I saw people who appeared more spiritually mature than I was as above me on the ladder. Somehow it seemed that they were closer to arrival than I was, closer to the kingdom where God was at work.

For some of us, a ladder may define our spiritual existence. We are held captive by the lie of comparison, and it feels as though we've got so far to go before God will be happy with our lives. There seem to be so many rungs to climb and so many things to change before we'll experience the kingdom. This thought can become incredibly defeating, and hope can seem fleeting.

But the kingdom of God is not the destination at the top of a ladder we climb. Rather, it's a realm that appears when we choose to engage. Any moment we choose God's way over our way, the kingdom breaks through. Whenever Jesus rules our day in any way, the kingdom breaks through. Anytime we choose to pray about a decision, to surrender to his will, to open the Bible for insight or wisdom, or to extend mercy or grace, the kingdom breaks through. Whether it's the first time or the hundredth time, in that moment Jesus reigns in your life, and the kingdom is at hand.

I find this shift in thinking to be so hopeful. God is always working in the now and the future, and we can choose to engage with his movement at any time. It's possible today, and it's possible tomorrow.

The kingdom is a paradox. To summarize what we discussed earlier, in Jesus' economy small is the new big. Jesus was clear that the first will be last and the greatest will be least. This may be the most difficult part to grasp—exchanging our view of success for God's view of success. The kingdom requires a different way of keeping score.

The same is true for our structured religion. It's interesting to me that so many of the things Jesus asks us to do are the very things that take away from a more structured and organized church. I'm not saying the kingdom and the church stand in opposition; I'm saying it's hard to prioritize both a heavenly realm and an earthly structure at the same time. This is the type of tension paradox brings.

Whenever we struggle to accomplish something spiritually, it might serve us best to take a moment and ask, Who does this serve? Is it me or the kingdom? I think we'll find it interesting how many things we do for the sake of our religion that have nothing to do with the kingdom. Some of them actually get in the way.

The kingdom is for sinners, not the righteous. We tend to hold a dichotomy in theology: although Christ died for us and offers us what we cannot earn, we still spend way too much time trying to appear like we earned it. This means that we either don't fully understand the doctrine of salvation or we still struggle with our identity in Christ, more specifically, how Christ truly sees us.

Jesus was clear, "For I have not come to call the righteous, but sinners" (Matthew 9:13). If we could somehow truly embrace and find comfort in the fact that we are sinners and that is where Christ meets us, it would change the reason we strive to be better. We would have an even greater appreciation for Christ and a truer love for mercy. We would desire the life change found in the freedom of unearned redemption, not debtor's guilt or insecurity.

The kingdom is more about letting go than holding on. The way we hold on to our expressions of religion is one of the greatest barriers to the kingdom breaking through in our lives. We become so consumed with our model or way of church, protecting our beliefs, and fighting over doctrine that we become distracted from what's most important.

Jesus addressed this in one of the greatest lessons about holding on, which is found in Matthew 16 just after Peter declared Jesus to be the Messiah:

> "And I tell you that you are Peter, and on this rock I will build my church, and the gates of Hades will not overcome it. I will give you the keys of the kingdom of heaven; whatever you bind on earth will be bound in heaven, and whatever you loose on earth will be loosed in heaven." (Matthew 16:18–19)

A close look reveals that as Jesus gave his marching orders, he never handed over the responsibility of actually building the church to Peter. That might seem odd at first, since Peter was the one he used to lead the church after Pentecost. But, Jesus clearly said that he himself would build the church. Instead, he handed Peter the keys to the kingdom. And his meaning was quite clear: what you do on earth has kingdom implications.

To be more specific, Jesus told Peter that whatever he held tightly on earth would be bound in heaven and whatever he held loosely on earth would be loosed in heaven.

It's not a surprise that it's the things we hold tightly that we are most likely trying to control or keep to ourselves. When we do that, whatever we are holding loses power. Conversely, whatever we hold openhandedly, what we don't control but surrender, is then loosed in heaven.

I believe the keys Jesus handed Peter represent the gospel, which is the foundation for the kingdom. As we seek to apply the gospel to any given situation, our goal should be to rightfully choose which things need to be unlocked and which things need to be bound.

If you're like me, right now you have something on your mind that you are begging God to intervene with or help you overcome. You need wisdom or insight to help you realize your hopes of seeing kingdom fruit. It's most likely these are the very areas in our lives we are holding onto too tightly. You may even be fighting for some incredibly good and worthy things. Quite possibly, they're no longer bound . . . but you're still holding on. Maybe this is your kingdom battle. Trust God with the result. Let go, and see what happens.

The kingdom is to be pursued. Jesus taught on just about every issue we can encounter. In Matthew 6 we see him teaching on giving to the poor, prayer, fasting, treasures in heaven, and worry. In essence he was teaching on mission, spiritual priorities, and religion, but people were so consumed and worried about their lack and God's provision that they were missing the point. So he took a moment to put things in perspective.

He reminded us that it's no more our job to worry about always doing the religious things right than it is to worry about how God is going to provide for our needs.

Our job? "But seek first his *kingdom* and his righteousness, and all these things will be added to you" (Matthew 6:33, emphasis added).

The kingdom is to be pursued. That means it gets our first efforts, not our leftovers once everything else is taken care of. We struggle when we get those priorities out of order. When we do this, we are no longer worshipping for the right reasons and no longer trusting God with our future.

> The kingdom is to be pursued. That means it gets our first efforts, not our leftovers once everything else is taken care of.

But remember that God loves us. He wants his very best for us. That is his will: that we experience his dream. And it's a far better dream than our dream. But when we first pursue religion and provision, we become consumed with those things instead of the things of the kingdom. This leads us to the wrong places and the wrong times with the wrong motives. In turn, we miss out on what God has in store for us.

TAKE HEART

As we wrap up our conversation, it's important to remember that it's the world that values the greatest . . . the highest . . . the ninety-nine sheep that did not wander off . . . the seen. Jesus, however, values the littlest . . . the lowest . . . the one . . . the lost. He isn't promising a kingdom without struggle. In fact, he made sure to remind us that "in this world you will have trouble." But along with the warning there's good news: "Take heart! I have overcome the world" (John 16:33).

Take heart! There is so much value in the small places of our lives: the work that seems invisible, the effort no one sees or notices, the quiet obedience that feels small when everyone else around you seems "big and important." Smallness is the substance of the gospel and the foundation of the kingdom.

Humility is honored in the heavens and attracts the very presence of Jesus. Rest assured, and do your work with joy and confidence.

Take heart! If you feel low or lost, if you feel like the one when the ninety-nine all seem to have their act together, happily milling around in their club, God rejoices over your search and rescue. He is for you and after your safe return. You are treasured and the cause for much holy joy. Look for your Good Shepherd, because he is looking for you. Be found.

Take heart, those of you who spend your life protecting and advocating for the vulnerable, for the little. Even when your work feels futile or frustrating or endless, when offenses have broken those you love and their healing seems elusive or impossible, you are doing the most important work of the entire kingdom. You have welcomed Jesus himself in, and according to him, you've filled your life with actual greatness.

Take heart! It is finished! The kingdom is here!

DISCUSSION QUESTIONS

1. Have you ever struggled understanding the difference between kingdom "now" and kingdom "not yet"?

2. Have you ever thought of a kingdom simply as a matter of rule? How does that idea help you understand areas in your life where there is a struggle for who is in charge?

3. In this chapter the author said, "The disciples still found their identity in their accomplishments and assignments instead of in Jesus himself." In your mind, how can identity affect our view of the kingdom?

4. Have you ever viewed faith or the kingdom as a ladder to climb? Why is that? Did that typically lead to more frustration or fulfillment as a believer?

5. How does considering the kingdom as a moment breaking through more than a ladder to climb change your view of daily faith?

6. Have you ever considered the kingdom implications of letting go and holding on? Why or why not?

7. In what ways have you held on to something to the detriment of the kingdom?

8. In what ways have you let go and seen the kingdom break through?

9. In this chapter we discussed how the kingdom is to be pursued. How are you doing in this department? What are two things you can begin to do to "seek first the kingdom"?

10. The kingdom comes with a cost. Where in your life have you felt that cost? How can the group be praying for you?

CHAPTER 7

A TRUER MISSION

*"You are the light of the world. A town
built on a hill cannot be hidden."*

—MATTHEW 5:14

EACH EASTER SUNDAY, my church does something unconventional. We cancel church. Instead, we have several projects throughout the city where we serve shoulder to shoulder with area nonprofits. We finish the day with the homeless community under the I-35 overpass with a brief Communion service followed by a huge hamburger grill-out and concert.

While our church structure has our people serving many of the same nonprofits regularly through their missional communities, Easter Sunday is just one example of how we help those newer to our church begin to understand the significance of mission.

Last Easter, we spent time serving with the River City Youth Foundation in an area of East Austin called Dove Springs, one of the most under-resourced regions of the city, with the highest crime rate. River City is a great organization that works closely with local leaders to provide community-building events and necessary services. They provide mentoring and after-school programs and open their facilities for kids to come and get help with homework, while also serving as the center of any area family events.

River City had a huge event planned for Easter Sunday but knew they needed a slew of volunteers. Although the number of volunteers they needed limited how many other projects we could do that year, we were thrilled they asked us to help.

It was an amazing Easter, a great day, when I met three unlikely people. The first was Buck. Buck is a young man who had just moved to Austin from Atlanta about a month before. He had come to the Dove Springs area in southeast Austin with his wife and six kids and was currently staying with extended family until they could get on their feet. I met him as we were setting up for the day.

Buck tapped me on the shoulder before the event even started. He needed a jump-start for his car. While I was helping him, he began to ask me about my tattoos and mentioned he wanted to find a good artist in the area to cover up the ones he got in prison. He wanted a new beginning, and Austin was his first attempt.

Later on in the day, while I was downtown, I met Stewart. Stewart was a cross-dressing homeless man with a beard, who claimed his last name was Little. He was a big ole stout dude, standing at least six foot four . . . wearing makeup . . . a dress . . . and panty hose.

This was the first time I'd seen Stewart at our downtown grill-out. He stood out like a sore thumb, so I began to engage him in conversation. He turned out to be about as nice a person as he could be. But my new friend did not come without cost. Since I was the one talking with him, I was the obvious one for him to ask for help zipping up the back of his flip-flop/flats hybrids that didn't fit right with pantyhose stretched between his toes. Awkward, to say the least.

Finally, I met a veteran named Ed. He, too, was homeless. He showed me pictures of himself as a youngster in Vietnam and carried his VA papers to prove he was a veteran. Since he was new to the streets and new to Austin, he shared how rough it had been at the homeless shelter downtown. Every moment he had looked the other way or fallen asleep, other people would steal from him.

Ed was a Christian and shared his boiling frustration with a church that was, in his words, "absolutely no help at all." His story was pretty heartbreaking. He had only been in Austin for a week and he needed help, but the church had not risen to the task.

It's easy to dehumanize these men, to judge them, and to categorize them as a seemingly less important class of people. It's also easy to find enough fault in their journeys to justify ignoring them. But as a good friend of mine always says, "It doesn't matter what you think. What matters is what Jesus thinks. And these are your brothers and sisters in Christ."

Why do I share these stories?

Every time I put another name and story to a face that I might normally just drive past, something changes in me. My arrogance is revealed and my misconceptions are exposed, and yet my fears and insecurities are erased. It somehow changes my spiritual scorecard. And it affirms in that moment that God is most certainly at work in me, in spite of me, and around me. This only increases as I engage need more deeply.

Jesus continues to shift, expand, confront, and grow my understanding of what it means to follow him, to be on mission with him. He was clear in Matthew 25 that when we serve the least, we ultimately serve him. I used to think that was the sole focus of this scripture, our goal being to serve Jesus, but I can't help but think there is an additional motive.

Everywhere we look there is physical, spiritual, emotional, and relational need. If we don't see it, we are either looking in the wrong places or we're not really looking. And the goal can never be just the event or program we're holding to fill that need. The goal must be the people we meet along the way. That's where we will find Jesus. He was clear that he'd be there, among the marginalized and broken.

Many of you are spiritually dry, some more than others. Some of you are fed up with a stagnant faith or with church as usual. Some of you recognize that you are a major part of the problem (me too). But most of you have one thing in common: you're simply looking for more of Jesus. There are many places where you might find him, but I know one place that you'll find him for sure: on the margins.

Buck, Stewart, and Ed changed me. Each of their stories

required me to view them differently than I might have had I not learned their names or taken the time to listen. I hope something shifted in them, also, in how they view the church. Regardless, I know something shifted in me.

This is the role of mission in our lives. Whether we're talking about missions, mission trips, or a missional posture, there is a sending element of the gospel that challenges us to break our religious norms and consider why we are where we are in any given moment.

We spend so much of our lives praying and searching for God's ultimate calling. We beg God to give us our purpose and fill our years with meaning. We yearn for a mission worth living for. Maybe we just need to delve deeper.

Trading a shallow religion for a deeper faith requires us to shift the way we view mission. True mission recognizes that where we are is where we've been sent. Mission is all around us. The people around us, the influence we have, and the places we go are our mission field. Our mission is to listen to people, steward our influence, and utilize our position to advance the kingdom.

That doesn't mean we have to lead everyone we meet to faith in Christ, but it does mean that we recognize and capture every moment as a gospel moment.

I would have never met Buck, Stewart, or Ed had I gone to normal church that day. I'm not telling you to skip church next Sunday. This could have been any day of the week that I broke away from my norm and placed myself in the same areas of town. What I'm telling you is that we have seven days in a week, and every moment is an opportunity.

LIVING ON MISSION

Living a life on mission means that we believe the gospel is the answer to any question, dilemma, or failure life has to offer. It means that we are constantly learning to surrender ourselves more deeply to this truth as we seek to lead others to the same.

> Living a life on mission means that we believe the gospel is the answer to any question, dilemma, or failure life has to offer.

The apostle Paul put it this way: "Be diligent in these matters; give yourself wholly to them, so that everyone may see your progress. Watch your life and doctrine closely. Persevere in them, because if you do, you will save both yourself and your hearers" (1 Timothy 4:15–16).

Jesus lived on mission.

In fact, Jesus coming to earth was a supernatural mission trip of sorts. In order to die for all mankind, Jesus first had to live for all mankind.

And that's what he did. Jesus put on flesh and moved into our neighborhood. He spoke our language and felt our pain. He experienced every temptation common to man and overcame. He walked among us, making sinners feel secure in his presence. He was an advocate for those who had no one to speak up for them.

Simply put, he lived his life for others. I can't think of a truer definition of mission.

We are created for this same mission. Each one of us desires some type of deep significance and purpose in life. That desire is rarely a superficial urge that is satisfied with secular success or quenched by power or position. It's a deeper kind of significance or purpose that we yearn for.

When we feel it, we know it.

It's that moment when God moved in a conversation with a neighbor, which you know you could never have fabricated. That time when a coworker called you for counsel in his darkest hour instead of his golfing buddies. That weekend when you met a homeless man and his story changed forever how you view the homeless community.

Those moments bring perspective, significance, and a reminder that God is at work ahead of us, around us, and through us.

Our job, as missional people, is to clear the clutter to allow the Spirit to move in those moments. It's to commit ourselves to a rhythm and lifestyle that places us firmly in the middle of possibility.

Mission simply means "sent." Missional people recognize that we are to be a "sent" people.

"Sentness" requires that we be sent from something to something else. We are sent from our comfort, from our living rooms, and from our church campuses, to community spaces where we reposition ourselves as believers in the hope of being invited into spaces where we can't invite ourselves.

For years the church has invited people in. And for years we've concluded that, while there are certainly some who come, an increasing number of people simply won't. Missional people attempt to live lives that are attractive to those who have no context for church. They earn their places in the lives of others.

Only then do they hold the moral authority or personal permission to speak truth into someone's life.

We don't compromise truth to appear attractive. In fact, it's quite the opposite. What's attractive about the lives of missional people is their posture and perspective. They ooze grace, so they are nonthreatening. They resonate hope and peace and understanding. This is the result of an increasing appreciation of what God has done for us. That's why it is so important that we understand God's grace and redemptive plan for each one of us. When we truly believe our guilt is taken away, our willingness to live on mission begins to outweigh our doubt and we become intentional about making ourselves available beyond the temple walls and the church campus. With the exception of theological understanding, this might be the most significant factor that will empower us to press deeper into a truer mission: simply the ability to truly say, "Here am I. Send me!" (see Isaiah 6:8).

What does that look like in our daily lives? Here are ten ideas to help you become more available. None of them have to do with what you do or don't do on Sunday mornings or with Bible study. Rather, almost all of them have to do with learning to be a good friend or neighbor:

1. Live in the now. Remember: where you are is where you've been sent. You are currently in your mission field. Right now. Right where you sit. We can become so distracted by what's around the corner and the next bigger thing that we miss every moment and opportunity today. Unfortunately, this is something that most of us struggle with and should probably commit to prayer daily.

2. Slow down and listen. Christians chronically talk too much. I think it's because we truly believe we have the answer. But we need to make sure we really listen to what others are saying and what others are asking. That's the difference between a person feeling like your friend or feeling like your project. Stop being a know-it-all.

3. Learn the names of your neighbors. This may sound elementary, but can you write down the names of your neighbors who live around you? Most people have six to eight houses in the neighborhood around their homes, but in my experience, most people can only name two or three of the families in those houses. It's a simple but critical step moving from "Hey, you!" or "What's up, bro?" to "Hey, Paul. How's Susie doing?"

4. Be normal. This is going to be hard for most of us, because we're not normal. The key is to stop trying so hard. Let the pressure off, and stop living as if someone's eternity depends on you. It doesn't. You just have the opportunity to help move him forward (or backward). The Spirit does the rest. Most disasters happen when we get too aggressive or pushy. Just be honest and vulnerable, and use normal talk. (Drop the Christian-speak and Sunday school answers.)

5. Lower your standards. I'm not talking about your personal standards. I'm talking about what you expect out of other people who don't share your faith. You can't hope to become a confidant to a nonbeliever if she feels judgment every time she does something you wouldn't do as a believer. Simply put, stop expecting others to live

by Christian standards when they don't hold Christian beliefs.

6. **Stop inviting people to church.** Instead, invite them to dinner in your home. If you're new to a neighborhood and you want to be the guy everyone avoids for the next twenty years, go ahead and let your first impression be you asking the question, "If you died tonight, do you know where you'd go?" A close second is handing the half-page mailer that your church put together about your next sermon series. Here's a question: When's the last time someone asked *you* about your faith or your church? Why do you think that is?

7. **Move to the front yard.** My friend Hugh and his wife deliberately sit on their front porch at 5:30 p.m. every day because they noticed that's when their neighbor comes outside to throw a ball with his dog. I have another friend who just walks the neighborhood each evening after dinner. Not only is it healthy; it's helpful. Every night he ends up having a conversation with a neighbor.

8. **Meet a need.** A few years ago, a neighbor moved in several houses down. I was struggling to find a way to say hello. I could never seem to catch him. Then one day I saw him pull up with a truckful of sod. Although he was trying his best, his son was too young to help effectively. I had nothing else to do. Spiritual dilemma ensued. You probably know how this one turned out.

9. **Keep it local.** This sounds a bit like a hipster thing to do, but why not stay local? Love where you live? Get to know business owners, staff, and other customers who frequent

local restaurants and businesses. I'm sure they'd appreciate your patronage. The more we do this, the more we'll see our relational paths cross, and you'll actually feel more a part of the local community.

10. **Be generous.** Whatever form it takes, be generous in your community when you can. That might mean with your money (maybe tip big when thinking about #9), it might mean with your time, or it might be with your physical resources. Open your home, open your calendar, and sometimes . . . open your wallet. A little goes a long way. Believe it or not, people *are* watching.

These are simple steps yet have a big impact. If we were to apply just half of these, I believe it would change the way Christians are perceived and would radically change the way we see mission.

MISSIONAL CHURCH

I've spoken with hundreds of frustrated church leaders and church attenders over the years who believe the structure of their current church keeps them from living on mission. But what we do on our church campus doesn't have to get in the way of mission. It should prepare us for mission.

We're called to love both God and our neighbor. We can lead an in-depth Bible study designed for believers and still live on mission. We can have a Sunday experience that is traditional and even liturgical and still live on mission. The only structure that will keep us from living on mission is if we are so busy doing church stuff throughout the week that we have no time to be present in our community.

For the last several years the church has been in deep conversation about how to become more and more mission-minded. We've recognized the dilemma that the very nature of gathering pulls resources, people, and time away from sending (and vice versa). I can't remember a time when the church was more committed to seeking God's best in understanding this tension and identifying where and how we fit into the mix.

To do this, we need to first recognize the key elements of our faith life and how church fits into them. For the sake of our discussion, let's consider three major categories into which you can pretty much subdivide anything we do because of our faith.

- Communion. This includes anything that places us in deeper relationship with God. Worship services, Bible study, prayer, small groups, and accountability groups all fit into this category. These things can be held on church campuses, in homes, or in the community. The location doesn't matter; what matters is our focus. Anything that places the focus vertically between man and God would fit into this category.
- Community. This includes anything that places us in deeper relationship with one another. It's the horizontal relationship fed by the desire to be known and includes any and all relationships, whether between believers or nonbelievers. This might be an event, a dinner, or just hanging out. Anything where building community or fostering friendships is the focus fits into this category.

- **Commission.** This includes anything that has to do with mission or our sending. It's the piece of us that is fueled by our desire for legacy and purpose. While this certainly includes the spiritual mission, it also includes any service of other people for whatever reason. It can be an act of benevolence, charity, or mercy. It can be a hand out or a hand up. Anything we do with purpose outside of ourselves fits into this category.

The majority of our existing church programming fits into the communion category. Our worship services, Sunday school classes, programs, home groups, prayer groups, and accountability groups all focus on communion with God. Likewise, the vast majority of our church staff responsibilities have to do with fostering communion. So it only makes sense that most of our outreach efforts have historically focused on inviting outsiders or nonbelievers to come to us and experience our church programs or events.

We spend the vast majority of our time, money, and efforts on the communion part of faith. We do this well in the existing church, which we should.

For a season we've attempted to break into the community category a little more by doing small groups in homes instead of on our church campuses. While I certainly agree it brings a different vibe to relationships among believers in the group, most of these groups' primary focuses are still on communion. So when we invite a neighbor, friend, or nonbeliever into the group, what he or she most likely experiences is Bible study (or some other Christian event/program) . . . just at a different place. We're seeking a different impact, but typically we fail to see the results we're hoping for. This has been frustrating for many.

I would argue that doing the same thing in a different location won't necessarily change its outcome or how it's perceived by visitors. That's not meant to be a stab at home Bible studies attempting to become outreach; it's meant to be a reality check for what we're really doing. We need to evaluate what we're hoping for and hold it up to exactly what we're structured to do. See if they match. Whether we're inviting people to our church campus or to our living rooms, if we're still inviting them in to experience a Christian communion of sorts—which includes necessary elements of church and faith—it's not mission.

In nearly every study I've seen over the past decade, somewhere around two-thirds of Americans say they would never attend church.

As we've struggled with the question of how to meet people where they are, I can't help but notice the difference between how we attempt to reach the two-thirds and how Jesus tended to reach people.

Jesus almost always met people at their greatest felt need as a part of addressing their spiritual need. He had amazing compassion that allowed him to see through people and speak their language.

Community and commission is that shared language between believers and nonbelievers. They speak directly to our common felt needs.

It's universally agreed upon by sociologists that each of us is born with an innate desire to know and be known.[1] That is the desire for community.

Similarly, I've never met anyone who at one point or another didn't feel a need for significance. College students struggle relentlessly with this as they choose their majors to coincide with their purposes in life. Empty nesters wrestle with this as they fight for legacy. That is the desire for commission or mission.

> Jesus almost always met people at their greatest felt need as a part of addressing their spiritual need.

Jesus knew exactly what he was doing when he met people at their felt need. He spoke their love language. The need was already perceived. Most people far from Christ do not perceive their own spiritual needs in the way we present it. While Jesus easily spoke their language, we might as well be speaking in Greek.

We tend to start with inviting outsiders to experience communion with God in the hopes of then connecting people in community and eventually sending them out on mission. But the math says this form of church will only reach the small percentage of people familiar with our current church culture. However, starting with community and commission with the hopes of moving people toward communion, by nature, meets the majority of people where they are.

It's important at this point not to take the Holy Spirit out of the equation. We all know God can and does work way beyond our sensibilities. We need to pray deeply for this and continue to press into it.

It's equally important to remember that no form of church is more significant than the other. We need both, the inward focus on communion and the outward focus on community and commission. But as we've discussed in the chapter on community and will see in the next chapter, on justice, we often focus on one at the expense of the other. And honestly, if we'd consider our gifts and experiences more deliberately, many of us would find that some of our frustration with the church is that we're neglecting where we might naturally serve best.

You may have gifts and abilities that lean more toward shepherding or pastoring, and you may love to sit in small groups, pray, and dig into Scripture. If you had to choose, you may choose a church focused on equipping the insider, the one-third. Or maybe you're the opposite. Some of you have more of an entrepreneurial spirit. It's likely you have more apostolic leanings and are more naturally drawn to mission and/or ministry to the outsider or outcast, the two-thirds.

We're all called to mission, but we're also called to steward our gifts and experiences. I'm convinced that Sunday church doesn't have to get in the way of mission. What you will find, however, is that mission will deeply impact your Sunday church. It's once again one of those intangible fruits of mission. Spend a week serving others, pouring into your neighbors, or connecting in your community, and I guarantee your worship experience will come with more depth. I've seen it and experienced it firsthand many times. Living on mission is the place where the dots of faith and life connect. Believer, I assure you: it's the sweet spot you've been looking for.

What if a huge part of the body of Christ synced their gifts and experiences with a commitment to church for the insider, another huge part of the body of Christ synced their gifts and experiences with a commitment to church for the outsider, and all of us committed to living on mission when we're not at church? We'd turn the world inside out!

DISCUSSION QUESTIONS

1. What has been your traditional view of mission?
2. Has this chapter changed that view? In what ways?
3. Regardless of your view of mission, how well have you been living it out?
4. In this chapter we learned that "true mission recognizes that where we are is where we've been sent." With this in mind, where do you see your greatest potential for mission?
5. What are two things you can do to begin to engage your new mission field?
6. How is living on mission different from serving through community? Which is more important?
7. For years the church has had a vision for inviting people to come to a church campus to experience Christ. How does your view of mission add or take away from this vision?
8. What are some important characteristics of a missional person? Which do you struggle with the most? Which are your strengths?
9. The chapter listed ten ideas to help you be more "available." Which one could you most identify with? Which presented you with the greatest challenge? Why?
10. As a missionary, how do you propose balancing the gospel and meeting felt needs? How did Jesus address need?

CHAPTER 8

A GROWING JUSTICE

He has shown you, O mortal, what is good.
And what does the LORD require of you?
To act justly and to love mercy
and to walk humbly with your God.

—MICAH 6:8

"BRANDON, COME HERE, quick!" a voice shouted from the hallway. "Tray duct-taped a kid to a tree!"

Not the words a youth pastor wants to hear in the middle of the night at youth camp. Especially when Tray is an adult volunteer and your best friend. Even more so after you had announced that anyone who bullies, teases, or pranks someone will be sent home on the next plane out.

Just two hours after having issued my warning, I walked outside the lodge at Glorieta Baptist encampment and saw that it was true. An eighth-grade boy named Matt was literally taped to a tree, with his feet dangling two feet off the ground. And Tray stood by, duct tape in hand, looking like a puppy who had just been caught going through the trash.

Matt was actually the reason I had given the speech earlier. He had a smart mouth that consistently put others down. Every word was negative. Every action was provoking. He was a bully and was targeting the smaller kids in the group for prank after prank. I even had a volunteer beg to go home after Matt put itching powder in his sleeping bag. Kids were crying, and Tray had had enough. So he taped him to a tree.

Matt got exactly what he deserved. He was a model student for the remainder of camp. Justice was served.

This is typically how we view justice, when someone gets what we think he deserves. Fortunately, it's not God's way of justice. Thank goodness. None of us want what we spiritually deserve.

Instead, God's justice brings healing. It's laced with a love for mercy. It sees broken things and restores them to wholeness.

Since God's form of justice is not our desired or natural form of justice, earnestly seeking justice requires a different game plan than what we're accustomed to. It requires us to become students again. Understanding how it fits into our everyday life and the gospel equation can be a process in and of itself, and if ever there was an area in which we need to learn and grow, it's the area of justice.

The prophet Micah presented the question, what is it that matters most to God? What is it that he actually requires of us? His answer: "To love mercy, seek justice, and walk humbly with our God" (Micah 6:8, paraphrased).

———

While it appears there are three distinct marching orders in his answer, justice is at the center of each of them. Loving mercy and walking humbly are inextricably linked with seeking justice. Loving mercy is the key motivation to justice, and personal humility is almost always the end result.

Maybe you're like me. I grew up in church. I mastered the Sunday school answers and at one point was king of the "Jesus juke." It was never a question whether we attended church every Sunday morning, Sunday night, and Wednesday evening. I knew where to go, what to do, and how to act. I knew what to say and what not to say to fit in. But I had no idea how to seek justice, much less nurture it so that it grows in me.

> Loving mercy and walking humbly are inextricably linked with seeking justice.

What I've found over the years is that most believers can identify with this. Most of us have spent the majority of our spiritual journeys in Bible studies and prayer groups and maybe once a year considering the world. We want to do good, but we either don't know what to do or can't figure out where to start. When we do begin to consider what difference we can make in the world, we are more likely to become paralyzed from the staggering statistics than moved into action. It can be overwhelming, and often we move from ignorance to paralysis.

But the key is to just do something.

I suggest starting with learning the theology behind justice as you begin simple acts of service wherever and whenever you can. From there, I promise you, it will grow—your understanding and your vision for what needs to be done, your awareness of what changes must happen, and your appreciation for how it relates to a holistic gospel. More than anything, you'll be amazed at how your mind and heart will begin to change.

WHERE DO WE BEGIN?

As humans, we tend to mess things up, so to give us a strong basis for our justice theology, we must first learn to seek justice for the right reasons. If our motivation is not correct, our results will rightfully seem off base. We'll hope for one end result and see another, possibly missing God, his kingdom, and most certainly his gospel at work. This would be a waste. We don't want to serve just to serve; we want to serve with a redemptive purpose in mind.

To do that, I'd recommend considering seven steps to seeking justice. Whenever I feel a bit off personally, I go back to this list and see where I've strayed from the course. The first four steps are primarily about learning. They are biblical and doctrinal concepts necessary to build the right foundation. From there, we'll discuss three simple steps to engage justice on a personal level. Let's get started.

Step 1: View the Journey as Discipleship

I've had the honor of serving in the local church for more than twenty years. The majority of those years I've spent my time developing systems to help people grow in their faith. We had different programs or events focused on outreach, different programs and events focused on discipleship, different programs and events focused on missions, and different programs and events focused on leadership development.

Each program and each event had a primary focus with a desired outcome. Outreach programs led people to faith. Discipleship programs helped people experience life change. And missions and leadership programs helped people see the big picture more clearly.

While these programs, in and of themselves, are necessary and helpful, I was amazed to realize how each of these desired outcomes is actually a natural consequence to seeking justice. When individual Christ followers pour themselves into a greater understanding and application of a biblical justice . . . people tend to come to faith, believers are transformed, they gain a new perspective, and they become some of the best leaders in the church.

I've spent years trying to program discipleship, and Jesus had the plan all along. Want to find Christ? You'll find him among the broken, the marginalized, the oppressed, and the abandoned.

Biblical justice is the point at which all the things of Christ come together in one beautiful and poetic moment. It's the moment when the scales fall off our eyes and we begin to see things differently. It's a discipleship environment that fills a gap that nothing else in our lives can fill. In my opinion, it's the tie that binds.

The first step in seeking justice is to somehow stop thinking of those we are serving as the project and start thinking of ourselves as the project. We have to first and foremost believe and hope that through our learning to serve and engage need, God is going to change the way we think and live. We need to go in as students of the ways of Christ knowing that we have a lot to learn. If we do, I guarantee: it will change things.

It will change our posture. If we're not careful, when we go to serve others, we can easily go in with pride. While it's natural to feel a little spiritually arrogant when serving others, it's important to know that it's most likely not coming from the right place. That is flesh, not spirit. When we're reminded that what we have is not of ourselves and when we consider God's goodness in our own lives, we will begin to gain the right perspective.

When we get this, our posture toward others will change. They are not the project; we are. God is ever molding us as we become the men and women of God he desires us to be.

It will change how we view success. I worked with a team who mentored a homeless single mom off the streets for more than a year, only to see her return to the destructive patterns that had landed her on the streets in the first place. She lost her kids to Child Protective Services and barely hung on to her government apartment.

Those who serve people on the margins are often exhausted, sometimes frustrated, and usually give up too soon. They feel like failures a lot of the time. Most people I've met who are working full time in nonprofit work have been doing so either for fewer than five years or more than twenty. Rarely do I meet someone between the five-and twenty-year marks. Why? It's hard to keep going. It's hard to constantly pour yourself into others when you're less likely to get the results you're hoping for than to seemingly fail.

The greatest way to stay encouraged and keep going is to remember that God alone holds the final result. Your success is determined by whether or not you've been faithful to do what God has called you to do. As I consider the team that worked with our homeless single mom, I realize that year changed their lives forever. It would have been easy to just throw up their hands and say it was a wasted year. But it wasn't. They were forever changed. Their hearts were changed. Their minds were changed. The way they viewed the homeless, single moms, and the poor were changed. And how they viewed God changed. Sounds like a home run to me.

It will change where we give credit. Either we get credit or God gets the credit for what we do. If it's us, Scripture is clear that we've received our reward in full. We shouldn't expect life change, joy, and future fulfillment from our efforts. If God gets the credit, the glory is his, and his favor is ours. It's at this point we will begin to see things differently. Our minds and hearts will be transformed, because we are allowing ourselves to be used by a God who makes all things new.

It will change you. Nothing has changed me more than learning a name and a story that goes with a face—especially a face of a person I usually simply think of as part of a people group. Whether it involved the story of a homeless man who lost everything he had, the face of an innocent teenage girl rescued from sex trafficking, or the names of two little orphans who now call our family their family, learning to seek justice has changed forever the priorities of my life.

Seeking justice is the ultimate perspective giver. It confronts materialism, consumerism, and individualism at the deepest levels. You know that thing you've fought all your life that you can't conquer? Yeah, that one . . . place your focus on the things of

Christ, and see what happens to it. I can only share from experience . . . no stone will remain unturned, and the Holy Spirit will pleasantly invade your life in the way you've always hoped.

Step 2: Settle Your Gospel Theology

We've discussed a holistic gospel fairly extensively in earlier chapters, so I won't repeat what we've already reviewed. I will, however, remind you that there is a strong tension that still exists in our culture between serving the least of these and the gospel.

Do the work now to settle your gospel theology regarding justice. There will come a day when you question whether or not what you're doing is truly connected. Most likely this will happen in a vulnerable moment when you feel you've failed or when what you're doing doesn't seem to be working.

Eventually, others will question your agenda and whether or not you've replaced a biblical gospel with a social gospel. It's important to remember that the gospel that saves is the same gospel that transforms and renews. This is the same gospel that is actively restoring all of creation. It's an active gospel that does not begin and end with salvation. It continues to work, heal, make new, shine light into the darkest places, and bring hope into the most desperate moments.

You can have confidence in this gospel. Press into it. Don't sell it short. Don't give up on it or embrace a shallow version of it. The gospel we know is a mile wide and a mile deep . . . if not even wider and deeper.

Too many Christians fail to experience the kingdom they see in Jesus' teaching. I believe with all my heart it's because their gospel theology is too simple. When we receive the gospel of salvation but go no further, all we have to look forward to is enduring this life as we hope for the Second Coming. There's not much hope in that for us while we're on this earth. But a holistic gospel invites us into God's amazing plan of redemption for all of creation now. It's at this place that the kingdom seems to break through and we get a glimpse of heaven on earth, his kingdom come. Now and not just later.

Step 3: Learn to Love Mercy

Jesus referenced the prophet's call to not only love mercy but to learn to love mercy (Matthew 9:13). He reminded us that he desires mercy even more than he does sacrifice. Jesus was dealing directly with our human bent to prefer physical offerings and sacrifices (or the modern-day checklist) as what we have to do to make God not mad at us.

But Scripture keeps pointing us instead to understanding God's mercy to the point where we not only appreciate it, but we love it.

How much do we really understand God's mercy? As we consider our lives, if justice were served, are we getting what we deserve? I would argue no. Most of us don't want what we deserve. We'd prefer God's mercy. The greater our understanding of God's mercy for ourselves, the more it will directly impact our ability to extend mercy to others.

This might take us doing some homework to fully ingrain it into our hearts. Before we begin serving others in need, maybe we need to spend a few hours or days considering our own failures that have been covered by the blood of Christ. Maybe we should consider how Christ's sacrifice does not run out of grace and mercy for us, regardless of how we continue to struggle in the flesh.

Maybe we need to be reminded of how the sinful woman in Luke 7 washed Jesus' feet with her tears and the most expensive of perfumes. While the others sat around and judged her for wasting such valuable perfume, Jesus understood what was going on with her.

> "Do you see this woman? I came into your house. You did not give me any water for my feet, but she wet my feet with her tears and wiped them with her hair. You did not give me a kiss, but this woman, from the time I entered, has not stopped kissing my feet. You did not put oil on my head, but she has poured perfume on my feet. Therefore, I tell you, her many sins have been forgiven—as her great love has shown. But whoever has been forgiven little loves little." (vv. 44–47)

This woman understood God's mercy. Her understanding did not come with arrogance and pride. It came with gratitude, humility, and a love for mercy.

Mercy is the biblical motivation for seeking justice. It's the fuel that fans the flame of action. When we are so in love with the idea of God's mercy in our lives, it's then—and only then—that we will have a true heart for justice.

Working backward, Jesus is saying if we don't have a heart for others, if we struggle with judgment or with someone deserving to be served, then maybe we do not fully understand what God has done for us. We do not yet have a love for mercy.

But when we develop a true heart for mercy, when we fully

understand that in God's goodness he has given us the right to be called children of God, our mercy will come without bias toward others. There will be no people group, no demographic, no label that would seem below us or beyond the reach of God's goodness.

Step 4: Gain a Biblical Definition of Justice

In the Hebrew language of the Bible, the definition of the word *justice* is "to be made right, restored."[1] Interestingly, the Hebrew word *tsedeq*, meaning "righteousness," is the same word used for "justice" (Psalms 89:14, 23:3).

Biblical justice is really about righteous restoration.

What's your definition of justice? Payback, retribution, punishment, or getting even? Often we speak of "getting justice," while the Bible speaks of "doing justice."

When we do or seek justice, our hearts are aligned with the truth of the gospel—which is that Christ died to make things right, to make them as they should be. Restored. When we act, participating in God's restorative justice, we begin to realize that this gospel is bigger than any weekend service project. We intuitively begin to move from a ministry of relief to a ministry of restoration, from a service project to a new way of living, from the heart of mercy to the desire for true justice.

Engaging justice includes increased awareness, followed by an intentional and sustained effort to confront need as it appears in global forms, such as the orphan crisis, human trafficking, or the need for clean water.

Mercy and justice together encompass the full biblical concept of serving the least. An expression of mercy quickly becomes an act of justice when a need is engaged with the hope of a long-term solution. Mercy offers compassion and relief. Justice offers an advocate and action.[2]

God is just. But his justice is expressed through his mercy. We see in the gift of Jesus the most perfect illustration of mercy translated into just action. God didn't have to send his Son, but he did because of his love and mercy. Our natural response to this is often that of a debtor, as if we could repay God. But that's not what he asks of us. He doesn't desire sacrifice; he's after something much deeper and more challenging than that. He wants our hearts.

> With what shall I come before the LORD
>> and bow down before the exalted God?
> Shall I come before him with burnt offerings,
>> with calves a year old?
> Will the LORD be pleased with thousands of rams,
>> with ten thousand rivers of olive oil?
> Shall I offer my firstborn for my transgression,
>> the fruit of my body for the sin of my soul?
> He has shown you, O mortal, what is good.
>> And what does the Lord require of you?
> To act justly and to love mercy
>> and to walk humbly with your God. (Micah 6:6–8)

Step 5: Learn to Identify Need

Probably the simplest and most mechanical step in seeking justice is to identify the needs in a specific community. Ironically, this is the place where most people get stuck.

Austin, Texas, has more nonprofit organizations per capita than any other city in North America.[3] There's a service project, volunteer opportunity, benefit event, or fund-raising race on every weekend of every month. While it can still be like herding cats to get a group of people involved in a specific opportunity to serve, it's pretty simple to find things to do in Austin.

A few years ago I spoke at a social justice conference in a city that has about one hundred thousand people living in the area. After the weekend I received an e-mail from an attender of the conference, claiming that his town wasn't like Austin and that they didn't have any nonprofits that he knew of in the area. He asked me for ideas on where to start.

I opened my laptop and Google-searched nonprofit organizations in his town. In .56 seconds there were about 374,000 results. I cut and pasted the URL into a reply e-mail and hit send.

While I know that maybe 100 or so of the 374,000 search results were probably true leads for opportunities to serve, I hope I made my point. You do know where to start. Sit down and put your head to it. Here are a few suggestions:

- Search the web for nonprofits in your town or city.
- Search the web for cause groups.
- Search the web for local benefits.
- Ask people on Facebook if they know of any needs locally.
- Meet with your local city officials to ask what the greatest needs are.
- Meet with your local school administrators to ask what their greatest needs are.

Last year we contacted the high school counselor in our upper-middle-class school district and asked if they knew of any specific needs around graduation. We quickly found out that there were thirty-eight graduating seniors who were considered homeless and could use sponsorships for caps and gowns, senior night, and other small needs that most seniors take for granted.

Maybe you live in a one-stoplight town. I don't know if I've ever stopped in a small-town gas station that didn't have an over-sized pickle jar near the cash register taking donations for a child or local family in need. Take a moment to ask the clerk how to get in contact with the family and help. It doesn't get any more personal and local than that.

> It's not that the need is not out there; it's that we haven't really looked.

The truth is that need is all around us. We've just conditioned ourselves not to see it. It's not that the need is not out there; it's that we haven't really looked. Put some effort into it, and keep trying. You'll be amazed at what you find.

Step 6: Encounter the Need

Once you identify needs in your community, choose one that includes something you can do, and do it. Pretty simple. Prepare yourself for a less-than-life-changing experience. People will disappoint you. It may not add up to what you thought it would. The organization may not be very organized, and you might feel as though you wasted a lot of time.

Breathe. Relax. And remember that this is not about fixing

the world. It's about being faithful to seeking justice. You, my friend, are being obedient. And you're learning.

You'll notice that this step is to *encounter* the need, to feel it firsthand. The next step is to engage need more deeply and through community. This is because everyone needs to go through a sifting process when it comes to serving. Some organizations won't fit you or your group. Some of you and your group won't fit some organizations.

We should always go into it with the attitude of "taste and see." Let's serve and then evaluate whether or not that was something we want to do more long-term.

When our home group contacts a nonprofit about serving them, we always ask, "If you had ten to fifteen people serving you in any capacity, what would it be?" Regardless of what they say, we'll do it. It may not be the coolest project on the planet, but you can rest assured that it's a job the organization actually needs done. That's a great way to start a relationship. If it doesn't seem to fit your group, then do it one time, learn from it, and move on to the next.

If you really want to serve an organization, don't come in with your own agenda. I promise you, you'll quickly become a volunteer coordinator's worst nightmare. Come selflessly with a desire to make a difference, and you will. You'll bless the organization, and you'll bless those you serve.

Step 7: Engage the Need in Community

Once you find an organization or cause that fits your group dynamic and passions, take a good look at your calendar, and think through your commitment. Be sure the group is on board and that it's not just a few individuals. That's a critical part of making it a sustainable relationship, especially if the nonprofit is not a faith-based group.

Here are three thoughts critical to your experience on engaging need.

Build relationships with the organization. Our church very intentionally serves with both faith-based and non-faith-based organizations. As long as we start with a common redemptive purpose, there is so much we can accomplish together. For example, what does it matter if it's a non-faith-based group if they are fighting for low-income families or orphans? Why not serve shoulder to shoulder with that organization, showing them that our God cares for what they care about? While our service is pointed toward the families in need, our ministry could be pointed toward the staff of that secular nonprofit. Some of the most fulfilling serving experiences can come through seeing a nonbeliever finally find hope in a church that comes to serve with him or her, and without an agenda.

Serve through community. It's really important as a part of the body of Christ that we serve through community. Not only does it bring purpose and mission to a small group of Christians who might normally just meet for Bible study and coffee, not only will it bring freshness and diversity into what you're doing as a group, not only will it deepen your relationships with those with whom you are serving, but when you serve together, it brings glory to God and the church. When we serve only as individuals, glory is more likely to be assigned to the individual.

Extend dignity. This might be the most critical thing we've learned over the years when it comes to serving. There will be a day when you question whether or not what you are doing is enough or how you're doing it is right. Someone else will always be doing more. And more than likely, you might even take some criticism that an act of charity or temporary relief is not impacting the long-term situation. It's true that giving a sandwich to a homeless man on one day is not going to end hunger on the streets of your city. But it will bless that man today.

We've been asked a number of times, "How do you know if what you are doing is right? In a world where sometimes our helping can actually and eventually 'hurt,' how do I know I'm serving the right way?"

Here's my answer: If, in how you are serving, you are extending dignity to the person you are serving, you are doing it right. You may not be solving a global issue, but you are modeling what Christ did for us.

For many of us, this means we need to get out from behind the other side of the table. For others it means we need to drop the matching T-shirts. There's nothing that says, "Hey, you're not one of us" more than matching T-shirts at a serving project. Hope that resonates.

THE BIG PICTURE

I'm not an expert on seeking justice. Personally, I've still got a long way to go. But I've never seen anything connect the dots better on this whole faith thing than serving the poor, taking up the fight for the orphan, or reorienting priorities around those on the margins. It's staggering how confronting, convicting, and revealing seeking justice can be. Maybe that's why it can be one of the most difficult things to get started and even more difficult to keep going.

Bottom line, it's just amazing how doing exactly what Jesus told us to do would not only be considered good news among believers and skeptics alike, but would be the most transforming thing for our own lives. It's almost as if Jesus knew what he was doing.

DISCUSSION QUESTIONS

1. How is biblical justice similar to or different from a traditional view of justice? Is this new to you? If so, how?
2. What is the difference between seeking justice and ensuring justice? How does this difference change your view on how you should be involved?
3. Why is it important that we start the justice conversation with theology?
4. We discussed how seeing the journey toward justice as a part of discipleship will change our posture, how we view success, and where we give credit. Why is this so important?
5. What is the difference between loving mercy and extending mercy? Why is it so important to start with loving mercy?
6. What are some ways you or your group can begin to identify need in your neighborhood, city, or state?
7. Does the idea of serving the poor initially give you a feeling of peace or of anxiety? Why is that?

8. How does the idea of dignity affirm or change the way you view service? Have you ever served someone in a way that may have stripped that person of his or her dignity? What would you do differently if you could?

9. Have you ever considered that God's idea of the church seeking justice is a bigger thing than just solving problems in the world? Why or why not? How has this chapter shifted your view on this?

10. On a scale of 1 to 10, how would you rate yourself on loving mercy and seeking justice? What are two things you can do to improve your rating?

CHAPTER 9

A FRESH PERSPECTIVE

*For the foolishness of God is wiser than
human wisdom, and the weakness of God
is stronger than human strength.*

−1 CORINTHIANS 1:25

IT WAS LIKE a surprise attack in the middle of the night. Texas had been in a drought for years, and although the spring came with consistent precipitation, no one expected the river levels to rise all that much. But in May 2015, more than seventeen hundred families suddenly found themselves displaced during the floods in central Texas. Homes and businesses were taken off their foundations, and dreams were swept away with the raging waters. Lives were lost, and hope was fleeting. It was devastating.

In the end, questions were all that remained. Where do we go from here? How do we rebuild? And, for many, how could a loving God allow such a horrible thing?

As believers, there are three ways we tend to respond to people wrestling with the spiritual aftermath of a natural disaster: (1) we prematurely stumble through an explanation of God's sovereignty, (2) we do our best to mobilize and help with cleanup and recovery, or (3) we do nothing.

Filled with questions of our own, our faith community chose to mobilize our people to help with cleanup and recovery. We were located just fifteen minutes from the heart of the devastation, and our plan was to fill needed volunteer positions to help clean up in lieu of our weekend worship services. I was thrilled to see not only our many church members, families, and small groups sign up, but also an outpouring of others from the community who decided to join our ranks.

It was a beautiful mix of believers and skeptics, of those who find refuge at church each Sunday and those who hadn't darkened church doors in decades. Differences in belief and other social issues seemed too petty not to set aside for such a catastrophe. This community needed as many people to help as possible.

Our plan was to work with the local disaster relief network, which operates as a collective point for churches throughout the Austin area. Their work primarily focuses on sustainable solutions, partnering with families, and developing a long-term plan for rebuilding. That specific weekend, they decided to pour all their energies into coming alongside another large nonprofit organization already on the ground and leading the way with recovery.

Everything was falling into place for the weekend. Then, I got the call.

"Hey, Brandon. This is Tray." (Yes, the same Tray who duct-taped a kid to a tree at youth camp). "Listen, I'm checking into this to make sure it's true, but I just heard that the organization we're partnering with is requiring *all* workers to sign a statement of faith before they can volunteer. Apparently, they are only letting Christians serve."

"That can't be true," I replied. "Make the calls, and find out for sure. It just doesn't make sense that at a time like this, anyone would turn away volunteers."

I hung up the phone with a sinking feeling in my gut. This wasn't the time for digging in our heels on doctrine. Surely this organization would make way for a diverse crowd from the community that was eager to help. This must be a misunderstanding.

Then Tray called me back.

"It's true," he said. "I heard it directly from them. They said they are having everyone wear matching T-shirts with their name on it and wouldn't let anyone serve who didn't represent the beliefs of the organization—more specifically, the beliefs of their founder."

"What's on the statement?" I asked.

"People have to sign off saying they are a Christian . . . something about the authority of Scripture, the Trinity, and . . . um, that they believe in the sanctity of marriage between a man and a woman."

My mind went straight to a conversation I'd had earlier in the week with a gay friend who had signed up to serve. There were many unbelievers who had been invited by neighbors, friends, and coworkers, who now, if they showed up, would be asked to sign a faith agreement before they could even shovel mud out of a widow's living room.

I was deflated.

I couldn't let our guests walk into this blind, so I sent out an e-mail letting them know what was ahead. While I chose my words to protect the organization the best I could, I made it clear that I didn't agree with the requirement. I asked those who could, with a good conscience, sign the statement to please stay the course. For everyone else, I apologized and told them we'd work around the clock to find other opportunities to serve.

Although we were eventually able to find two other, smaller projects to point our people to, this experience totally took the wind out of our sails. Of the hundreds who had signed up, fewer than twenty showed up to serve the original organization. It was a very disappointing weekend.

Each of you reading this story is probably responding from a different perspective. Some of you instantly empathize with the organization trying to stay true to their beliefs. You understand the constraints that come with managing an organization, as well as the foundations on which infrastructure is built. Your natural instinct is to see the truth they are trying to protect.

Others of you are offended by the experience. You may naturally see things through the eyes of the nonbeliever, the one who might be served, or the believer who invited a skeptic friend, viewing this as an example of a bigger problem in the church.

Both perspectives come from a seemingly good and hopeful place—in this case, one side holding to truth, the other holding to grace. But as each side considers the other, the criticism seems just as obvious. One side seems too legalistic and the other too compromising.

Horace Walpole wrote, "This world is a comedy to those that think, a tragedy to those that feel."[1] And indeed, it's very common for two people to experience the same thing yet see it differently. This has been the source of a lot of tension among believers. Everything we do—from worship to discipleship to missions and justice work—is affected by our perspective.

Since application is the goal of interpretation, it is necessary work to do a little soul-searching about *why* we believe or see things the way we do. We must evaluate our biases if we are to live truly gospel-centered lives. To do so we must first understand where these biases came from. Let's start by taking a look at our formative *faith environments* and our past *experiences with friends and family*.

Faith Environments

When it comes to interpreting how we apply Scripture, nothing influences us more than the faith or church environment in which we were raised. While there are ongoing arguments among sociologists on whether or not certain foundational behaviors are due to nature or nurture, one thing is for sure: both are significant. We can't control nature, but we have everything to do with nurture.

For example, we've all struggled with balancing grace and truth. Most likely that's because we grew up in faith environments that may have unknowingly or unintentionally valued one over the other. But if we were to truly live like Jesus, our struggle would not be to balance grace and truth; the struggle would be to be full of both. John 1:14 says, "The Word became flesh and made his dwelling among us. We have seen his glory, the glory of the one and only Son, who came from the Father, full of grace and truth."

Being full of both grace and truth is part of his glory revealed. It's not a balancing act. The goal is to max out both, neglecting neither. This fullness defined Jesus, yet our pendulum tends to swing a mile to the left or a mile to the right, depending on what our formative faith environment emphasized.

Very few of us have been nurtured toward both. Some of us grew up in a truth-focused faith environment or church. Typically, these environments value doctrine over method or, at the bare minimum, focus more on Scripture, study, and obedience than on understanding freedom and grace. While this environment may result in a more developed view of a doctrinal gospel, it often lacks the ability to empathize appropriately during a situational or social issue. Our default becomes a form of legalism, and our confidence is often misinterpreted as arrogance or even judgment.

Conversely, some of us grew up in a grace-focused faith environment or church. Typically, it is these "it's the heart that matters" environments that often value the how over the what. The life that accompanies this focus is often expressed outside the walls of a church service or Bible study. Our default is grace, at times seemingly at the expense of truth, and our freedom is often misinterpreted as being too compromising.

Those of us who grew up in truth-focused environments most likely struggle with extending grace to ourselves and others.

Those of us who grew up in grace-focused environments most likely struggle with applying truth to ourselves and others.

And so we clash when we come together to pursue gospel living, not always realizing the reason we see things so differently. What can we do about this? Knowing where our roots lie is a great place to start. From there we can ask the questions, *Do I need to apply more truth to this situation, issue, or relationship, or do I need to extend more grace?* and, *How is my perspective perhaps skewed by my faith environment background?*

Knowing where we default could be a game-changer for how we forever view other people, biblical issues, and personal struggles. Once we have a clearer picture of our own tendencies, we'll be able to better take a step back and impartially seek God's direction and point of view.

Friends and Family

We are all drawn in one way or another to the idea of tribe. Simply put, we all want to belong. This might be the most obvious of the influencers of bias but the most difficult to overcome. Often our desire to belong informs our beliefs more than it should.

There are many ways the idea of belonging can negatively impact our view of truth, but two in particular on each end of the spectrum probably affect the greatest percentage of us: (1) fear of rejection, and (2) hope for acceptance.

In any group, the natural tendency is for individuals to adopt the majority opinion or belief. Those who were on the fence get the affirmation and confidence they need from the group to fully adopt an idea they were previously unsure about.

The more they believe the same things, the more safely they remain in the tribe.

We see this phenomenon develop early on within families. That is why children tend to stick pretty closely to the viewpoints their parents have. And it's the same for various friend groups or communities that informally hold to some general common beliefs.

The problem comes when there is continuous disagreement in belief, whether it be when a child is starting to develop his or her own opinions or a member of a community is leaning more and more away from the previously established ideas about one thing or another. Eventually this becomes a source of contention that threatens an individual's position in the group—especially if his or her dissenting viewpoint is beginning to make sense. At this point, the individual either becomes countercultural to his or her most significant relationships, or submits to the majority out of a fear of rejection.

There have been a number of social issues over the past several decades that came with incredible tension just before the tipping point of a major change in belief. In that tension was a lot of personal searching and counting the cost. I have met with dozens of people who have begun to question their convictions on an issue, yet feel they could never admit their doubts to their tribe for fear of being rejected or ostracized. The desire for belonging over belief is nearly impossible to navigate. Bottom line, most people either willingly or subconsciously go with the crowd.

This undoubtedly has a lot to do with why early adopters are like pioneers heading west, a small group of people with big ideas and unsure results. If we've learned anything from history, the crowds will come along later once they see the landscape as a little safer.

Another perspective related to belonging is what I call a hope for acceptance. I first noticed this as a young pastor when people would visit from a crosstown church. While I had decided years ago that every city needs a diverse church and that not every church is for everyone, it quickly became evident to me that some people were unsure of why they needed a change. Instead of saying what they really liked about our church when visiting, they would say something negative about the church they were leaving. This came from an outdated assumption that all churches are in competition for members and that somehow a negative comment about the competition would make the visitor more welcome.

Honestly, that's just weird to me. But it really happens. It's a classic thing we do when we want to be accepted by a new group. Our desire to belong overrides our desire to do what is right.

Whether it's fear of rejection or hope of acceptance, our desire to belong truly affects our belief, or at least what we appear to believe. To gain a fresh perspective on any of the issues we've discussed, it's important that we reconsider how much we value our place in our tribe and how much we allow that to color the way we think about things.

The key is to deeply consider whether or not our stance on any specific issue is truly informed and prayerful or simply a reaction to what we've experienced. If our desire is to *know* the truth and not just to be right, this would be well worth our time to consider.

With that in mind, let's evaluate our current perspective while the idea of faith, friends, and family is fresh in our minds. Think about a current issue or situation you're dealing with. Now, considering your historical bias, ask yourself a few questions:

- Do I have an unconscious bias on this topic, or can I view this fairly?
- Is my view on this topic biblical, or is it cultural? Is it something studied or experienced? How should that inform how I move forward?
- Am I using Scripture to defend my belief or to define my belief?
- Is my view protecting my place among my friends, or is it proclaiming the gospel?

These questions aren't going to unlock every issue or truth you're struggling with. But if we'll contemplate them honestly and prayerfully consider our answers, we'll move in the right direction.

BUT, REALLY, AM I RIGHT?

George Carlin once jokingly said, "Some people see the glass half full. Others see it half empty. I see a glass that's twice as big as it needs to be."[2]

Maybe the problem at the core of our differing viewpoints on various issues is that we're still stuck looking at the coin as two-sided. Perhaps there's a fresh perspective we need to regularly consider. Is it possible that in our search for truth and our desire to be right we've neglected the most important perspective of all? A third perspective . . . God's perspective?

Sometimes it's good to be reminded that God's ways are simply higher than ours and we can only expect a certain level of understanding. The rest is just faith. For some reason, that always brings me a certain level of peace.

The apostle Paul put it this way:

> Where is the wise person? Where is the teacher of the law? Where is the philosopher of this age? Has not God made foolish the wisdom of the world? For since in the wisdom of God the world through its wisdom did not know him, God was pleased through the foolishness of what was preached to save those who believe. Jews demand signs and Greeks look for wisdom, but we preach Christ crucified: a stumbling block to Jews and foolishness to Gentiles, but to those whom God has called, both Jews and Greeks, Christ the power of God and the wisdom of God. For the foolishness of God is wiser than human wisdom, and the weakness of God is stronger than human strength. (1 Corinthians 1:20–25)

Paul was calling us back to the way of God, reminding us that God's foolishness (as if there were such a thing) is greater than our wisdom. It's an age-old perspective that has never changed. Yet each time it overtakes our perspective, it brings freshness to our understanding. It's a way that breathes life into dry bones, one that places us deeply in the middle of his redemptive story.

———

In order to exchange a shallow religion for a deeper faith, we need to return to the beautiful journey of searching for the heart of God, of seeing through his eyes. We need to repent of our pride and our selfish search for truth and our own agenda, replacing them with the mind of Christ. We need to throw out the ways that tear down and divide and seek the Spirit's leading toward being agents of the gospel that restores and renews. Because somehow, in his way, truth convicts and corrects, and grace brings freedom rather than bondage and fear.

> In order to exchange a shallow religion for a deeper faith, we need to return to the beautiful journey of searching for the heart of God, of seeing through his eyes.

WHAT MATTERS MOST

So what exactly is the mind of Christ? What is this third perspective that is outside of our naturally built-in points of view? It's amazing how simple truths evade us. Even the most obvious or overstated words of Jesus that ring true in our minds and souls are often misapplied in an everyday faith, even the things that matter most. There's no truth more simply stated than the command to love God and love others. It all comes down to love.

To leave no doubt, Jesus, when asked point-blank what the greatest commandment in the Law was, replied:

"'Love the Lord your God with all your heart and with all your soul and with all your mind.' This is the first and greatest commandment. And the second is like it: 'Love your neighbor as yourself.'" (Matthew 22:37–39)

But He didn't stop there. He went on to say:

"All the Law and the Prophets hang on these two commandments." (v. 40)

The word *hang* here is from the Greek verb *kremannumi*, which means, "suspend." Jesus is not only saying that loving God and loving others is the first and most important (and revealing) thing we can do, but that these two principles are the cables on which all the laws are suspended. Like the cables on a suspension bridge, literally holding up the massive structures below, loving God and loving others hold up the Law and the instructions of the prophets.

Without them, everything comes crashing to the ground and is rendered useless, even destroying those caught below in the rubble. Without them there is no bridge. No way. No hope.

This isn't the only place where Scripture calls us to return to the suspending power of loving God and others. Let's take a moment to return to the Ten Commandments.

And God spoke all these words:
I am the LORD your God, who brought you out of Egypt, out of the land of slavery.
You shall have no other gods before me.

You shall not make for yourself an image in the form of anything in heaven above or on the earth beneath or in the waters below. . . .

You shall not misuse the name of the LORD your God, for the LORD will not hold anyone guiltless who misuses his name. . . .

Remember the Sabbath day by keeping it holy. . . .

Honor your father and your mother, so that you may live long in the land the LORD your God is giving you.

You shall not murder.

You shall not commit adultery.

You shall not steal.

You shall not give false testimony against your neighbor.

You shall not covet your neighbor's house. You shall not covet your neighbor's wife, or his male or female servant, his ox or donkey, or anything that belongs to your neighbor. (Exodus 20:1–17)

Did you catch it? I read the Ten Commandments for years before I realized there are two very distinct focuses in the list. The first four commandments focus on a vertical relationship between us and God. In these verses, God not only reminds us what he's done for us; he reminds us that he is *for* us, that he is jealous for us, and that he wants his absolute best for us. Translated, he desires that we understand how deep his love runs for us. It's the first love, the one that fuels all other love. While it's written as the law, it's like a love letter of what's to come, and it's signed "Love, God."

What about the rest of it? Did you notice what happens?

After the first four commandments, focused on loving God, we see a distinct shift in attention. We move from vertical to horizontal, from how we view and interact with God to how we view and interact with others. Six commandments all focused on how we live, respect, and love one another.

Or, as Jesus put it, love God with all you've got, and love your neighbor as yourself. It's not a new command. It's just the heart of the law that's been there all along.

In the Sermon on the Mount, once again, Jesus focused on two perspectives. The first several of the Beatitudes address our posture before God: recognizing our spiritual poverty, mourning our sin, practicing meekness, hungering and thirsting for righteousness. Then he wrapped up the list with a new posture toward others: extending mercy, practicing purity, being peacemakers, and living righteously.

Scripture consistently gives us the mandate to navigate how we love God and others. It's the heart behind everything we've discussed and the lens through which we must constantly look to live out the gospel well. What does it mean to truly love God and truly love others, to see all of our choices and actions through the lens of this love, this third way? For most of us, it means seeking a new or fresh perspective on both.

A Fresh Perspective on Loving God

We live in an age of grace. We have the amazing honor of walking this earth between the first and second comings of Christ. We live under the new covenant of Christ's sacrifice. We learn, live, and worship in faith of a loving God.

Yet many of us still live in fear of the God of the old covenant.

We are like the people of Israel after Moses came down the mountain with the Ten Commandments:

> When the people saw the thunder and lightning and heard the trumpet and saw the mountain in smoke, they trembled with fear. They stayed at a distance and said to Moses, "Speak to us yourself and we will listen. But do not have God speak to us or we will die." (Exodus 20:18–19)

The Law was given by God, that we might clearly see our need for a Savior. The Savior was given that we might clearly be declared innocent before God.

> For all have sinned and fall short of the glory of God, and all are justified freely by his grace through the redemption that came by Christ Jesus. God presented Christ as a sacrifice of atonement, through the shedding of his blood—to be received by faith. He did this to demonstrate his righteousness, because in his forbearance he had left the sins committed beforehand unpunished—he did it to demonstrate his righteousness at the present time, so as to be just and the one who justifies those who have faith in Jesus. (Romans 3:23–26)

Even in the Ten Commandments, which were designed to expose our sin, we see the heart of a God who is jealous for us and who wants his best for us. If that's not convincing enough, then remember the invitation of Jesus . . .

"Come to me, all you who are weary and burdened, and I will give you rest. Take my yoke upon you and learn from me, for I am gentle and humble in heart, and you will find rest for your souls. For my yoke is easy and my burden is light."
(Matthew 11:28–30)

It's nearly impossible to shift our view of the gospel, identity, discipleship, community, kingdom, mission, and justice without shifting how we view and approach God. Each requires a dependency and confidence that can only come from knowing you're a child of the King. Without these, we'll remain like the beggars outside the city gates, simply hoping for scraps.

A Fresh Perspective on Loving Others

Jesus spent more time teaching his disciples about how to live among others than he did anything else. They lived in a day when you could be killed for making a wrong claim about faith, and they were confronting the most difficult of legalists, the kind with actual political power. To say they were at risk is a massive understatement.

With varying politics, current racial tensions, social variables, and, of course, religious beliefs, today there are more lines that divide than there are ties that bind.

But it's not supposed to be easy. In fact, our love of one another is the greatest measure of our faith, and Jesus set a major precedent for how we were to proceed. No one in the history of the world introduced a more radical and fresh perspective on how we are to view others than Jesus.

The Outcast

Immediately following the Sermon on the Mount, Jesus had everyone's attention. It was the first sermon of his public ministry, and the crowds were pulsing with anticipation after hearing this new teaching. Everyone was watching for his next move.

Jesus knew they were watching. He knew whatever he did next would be significant for all who would follow him. Even for us today.

> When Jesus came down from the mountainside, large crowds followed him. A man with leprosy came and knelt before him and said, "Lord, if you are willing, you can make me clean."
>
> Jesus reached out his hand and touched the man. "I am willing," he said. "Be clean!" Immediately he was cleansed of his leprosy. Then Jesus said to him, "See that you don't tell anyone. But go, show yourself to the priest and offer the gift Moses commanded, as a testimony to them." (Matthew 8:1–4)

In the realm of unclean human conditions, leprosy was the worst. It was indicative of sin and deeply linked with character defect. A person with leprosy was rendered unclean forever.

Yet Jesus saw him, reached out to touch him, and healed him.

You see, just after he taught the most significant sermon in the history of time, Jesus didn't make his way to the next sanctuary to meet with the religious. He made his way to the next street corner to meet with the outcast.

By meeting him in his greatest need, Jesus restored more than this man's health; he restored his dignity. Then he instructed him to go directly to Jerusalem, be examined, and get ceremonially clean. Why? To have him restored to the communion of the church from which his leprosy had separated him.

What if every believer in every city was committed to welcoming in and restoring the outcast of their communities, like this leper? Jesus saw to it that he was restored spiritually, relationally, emotionally, and physically. Then he sent him to the temple as a testimony to the religious. Jesus used the weak to lead the strong.

Jesus gave us a new kingdom that came with a new perspective. This radical perspective was fueled by compassion for the outcast.

The Outsider

But he didn't stop there. From there he went to Capernaum.

> When Jesus had entered Capernaum, a centurion came to him, asking for help. "Lord," he said, "my servant lies at home paralyzed, suffering terribly."
>
> Jesus said to him, "Shall I come and heal him?"
>
> The centurion replied, "Lord, I do not deserve to have you come under my roof. But just say the word, and my servant will be healed. For I myself am a man under authority, with soldiers under me. I tell this one, 'Go,' and he goes; and that one, 'Come,' and he comes. I say to my servant, 'Do this,' and he does it." (Matthew 8:5–9)

Israel was under Roman occupation, and the centurion was a Roman officer. He had all the power the leper lacked, but he was not Jewish. He was an outsider of the faith with a resented position of authority.

If Jesus' compassion for the leper shocked people, then this one made them lose their minds.

"I will go and heal him," Jesus said.

Notice that the soldier did not make one qualifying statement about his belief system or social preferences. And there was no mention of his being deserving or undeserving. All we see is that he had *faith*.

> "Just say the word, and my servant will be healed," he answered.
>
> When Jesus heard this, he was amazed and said to those following him, "Truly I tell you, I have not found anyone in Israel with such great faith. I say to you that many will come from the east and the west, and will take their places at the feast with Abraham, Isaac and Jacob in the kingdom of heaven. But the subjects of the kingdom will be thrown outside, into the darkness, where there will be weeping and gnashing of teeth." (Matthew 8:10–12)

His mercy is also for the outsider. Why? This outsider acknowledged Jesus' divinity and his authority. In response, Jesus ascribed to a Gentile oppressor the "greatest faith in Israel."

We have a lot to learn from Jesus' perspective. He chose the most outcast-iest outcast and the most outsider-ish outsider.

Jesus used the word picture of a feast in this scripture, one that is often used when describing the kingdom. Here he was saying that many who consider themselves *insiders*—who expect a place at the table—will come to the table but not find their seats. But this man, the outsider, will have a place. What does this teach us? Invites are not restricted anymore to a particular nation or set of people; it's by faith that we are invited.

Jesus sets a big table. He changes the question from "Who is out?" to "Who is in?"

To our knowledge, this man was most likely still a Roman centurion the next day. This makes me uncomfortable. We like people to share our theology, skin color, practices, politics, health, views, and interpretations, but what about when folks fall way outside those lines? Answer: that is not our responsibility. It's Jesus'.

It's not ours to determine how God extends salvation on planet Earth. We don't have one clue how Jesus makes insiders from outsiders. He's been doing it for centuries, redeeming humanity, and not in the safe little evangelical way we understand it in America. Our job is simply to love.

The Insider

Despite all his regard for those on the outside, Jesus still does not forsake his people. On the third strategic encounter in a row, we see his mercy extends also to the insider.

> When Jesus came into Peter's house, he saw Peter's mother-in-law lying in bed with a fever. He touched her hand and the fever left her, and she got up and began to wait on him. (Matthew 8:14–15)

Jesus is for the person who loves and understands the Bible. The person who's been around church a long time. The person who has sought him his whole life.

To be honest with you, I've felt more like an outsider than

an insider to the mainstream church crowd over the past several years. I find myself being pushed to the margins more and more. I'm drawn to those who are broken, oppressed, and marginalized. So it's a great reminder to me personally to see that Jesus still loves the insider just as well.

Because sometimes I don't.

The insider is the most difficult person for me to extend grace to. Maybe this is because I've been one most of my life.

> Jesus' people are made up of everyone. He loves near and far, the normal and the weird.

I've judged others while struggling with private sin. I've deflected, accused, and pointed the finger. And I realized I still do that from the outside. It's just that now my arrows are pointed in.

This scripture convicts me as I write this chapter. I tend to reject the insider.

But Jesus' people are made up of everyone. He loves near and far, the normal and the weird. If we are Christ followers, loving as Jesus loved, including who he included, then we also need to set a wider table. None of us are better or worse, or more or less worthy, likely, and welcome.

We celebrate that truly when we can confidently say we are saved by the grace of Jesus, not one thing of ourselves.

THE BEGINNING AND THE END

Before we end our conversation, let's take a moment to jump back to the very beginning of this book where we discussed the story of the woman caught in adultery. Jesus was put in the situation where there seemed to be only two obvious perspectives and outcomes: either she was guilty or she was innocent. Jesus took a new posture and introduced a new perspective, which resulted in a new option: grace. It was as brilliant a moment as it was beautiful.

There's a common thread in each chapter of this book that changes everything. It's not just the existence of Jesus, since we know that Jesus existed from the beginning. It's the way and the life of Jesus that changes everything. He literally embodied faith, hope, and love.

His life offered a new way of doing the most sacred and ancient of things. He reminded us that we need new wineskins to fully preserve and enjoy the wine. He offered a third option that can be as much about the why and the how as it is about the what.

Whenever in doubt, may we always return to Jesus. That's the foundation of trading a shallow religion for a deeper faith. Whether we're talking about how we do church, how we deal with sin, or how we view ourselves, may we never be content with the first glance. Instead, may we hunger for the depths, may we search for the pearls, and may we seek first his kingdom.

DISCUSSION QUESTIONS

1. While most people tend to lean more naturally toward one or the other, Scripture calls us to be full of both grace and truth. Which comes most naturally to you?

2. We discussed how our early faith, friends, and family influence our spiritual perspective. Which one would you say has shaped your belief perspectives the most?

3. In what ways have your perspectives changed over the years? Why? How have your perspectives stayed the same or even strengthened? Why?

4. We've discussed at length how the gospel changes the way we should view ourselves. What are some of the perspective changes Jesus taught regarding how we view and treat other people that are new to you or that you need to work on?

5. Has the desire for belonging ever influenced your believing? In what ways? Did this end up having a positive or negative effect on your faith?

6. Have you ever struggled with the balance between seeking truth and seeking to be right? How did this impact your posture or perspective with the other person involved? Would you say you did it intentionally or unknowingly?

7. Are you a person who typically sees truth as black-and-white (like a two-sided coin)? In your mind, how has this impacted your ability to see God's perspective? Good or bad?

8. The apostle Paul reminded us that God's foolishness is wiser than man's wisdom. While this is a statement about God's mind, how should or could this reality change your heart?

9. Have you ever noticed that the Ten Commandments and the Beatitudes were written with the same two perspectives (loving God and loving others) as what Jesus said were the Greatest Commandments? How does this change or affirm your view on how important our posture and perspective are regarding other people?

10. In this chapter we discussed the outcast, the outsider, and the insider. Which do you identify with the most? Which do you struggle to identify with the most? Why?

ACKNOWLEDGMENTS

HOW COULD I ever write a list of acknowledgments without starting first with my amazing family Jen, Gavin, Sydney, Caleb, Ben, and Remy. You each inspire me and challenge me as I attempt to be the husband and dad I hope to be. I love you deeply.

To Bryan Norman at Alive Literary Agency. Thanks for believing in me, for believing in this project, and for getting it into the hands of those who continued to believe in me and this project. Blessings to you on your new endeavor as president at Alive.

To the #4500. You guys are amazing. Your encouragement, Facebook posts, and e-mails made this book worth it even before it came out. Thank you to the moon and back.

To Brian Hampton, Jessica Wong, Stephanie Tresner, Janene MacIvor, Sara Broun, Jeff James, Aryn VanDyke, and the team behind the team at Nelson Books. Thank you for making an author feel valued and worthy and like they've got something to say. You are family to the Hatmaker family.

To my faith community at ANC. Thank you for being the space where I can lead and learn at the same time. Thanks for your grace, your encouragement, your constant love, and for staying with us on the constant journey of *becoming*.

To my friends Tray and Jenny Pruet, Trace and Shonna Shelton, and Jason and Alison Morriss. Thanks for always being a sounding board (even when your ears run out of words), for processing life together, and for living shoulder-to-shoulder with us in the trenches.

To the Grim Guardian Motorcycle Club. You guys are crazy. Thanks for constantly expanding my understanding of what love and brotherhood can mean. Much LL&R.

To the Supper Club crew, Aaron and Jamie Ivey, Brad and Noelle Otts, and Nate and Melissa Navarro. You keep making the Hatmaker books, there's a reason for that. Thanks for making us feel normal. Although none of us are normal.

Finally, to my dad and mom, Bob and Jacki Hatmaker. Mom, you've showed me what a warrior looks like through your years of constant prayer and unshakable faith. Dad, you're the strongest, most loyal, and committed man I know. You've shown me what believing can look like outside the walls of normal religion. Thank you both. Jesus said that others will recognize his disciples by their love. You've both loved me so deeply.

NOTES

Introduction

1. Entry from May 11, 2011: "A Mile Wide and an Inch Deep," BarryPopik.com, accessed January 11, 2016, http://www.barrypopik.com/index.php/new_york_city /entry/a_mile_wide_and_an_inch_deep.

Chapter 1: A Fuller Faith

1. "Matthew Henry: Commentary on Matthew 13," Blue Letter Bible, accessed January 11, 2016, https://www.blueletterbible .org/Comm/mhc/Mat/Mat_013.cfm.

Chapter 2: A Bigger Gospel

1. Tim Keller, "The Gospel in All Its Forms," *Leadership Journal,* Spring 2008, http://www.christianitytoday.com/le/2008 /spring/9.74a.html.

Chapter 3: A New Identity

1. Jeff Vandersteldt, "You Do Who You Are," the Gospel Coalition, October 7, 2014, http://www.thegospelcoalition.org/article /you-do-who-you-are.

Chapter 4: A Deeper Discipleship

1. Toby Keith, "As Good as I Once Was," by Toby Keith and Scotty Emerick, recorded 2004–2005, on *Honkytonk University*, DreamWorks Nashville, album.
2. Mobile Loaves & Fishes, "What We Do," MLF.org, accessed January 13, 2016.

Chapter 5: A Better Community

1. Stephen Covey Quotes, BrainyQuote, accessed January 13, 2016, http://www.brainyquote.com/quotes/quotes/s /stephencov450798.html.

Chapter 6: A Closer Kingdom

1. Marcus Dods, "Necessity of Becoming Like Little Children" (commentary on Matthew 18:1–14), Bible Hub, accessed January 13, 2016, http://biblehub.com/sermons/auth/dods/necessity_of _becoming_like_little_children.htm.
2. *Matthew Henry's Commentary on the Whole Bible*, commentary on Matthew 18, Bible Hub, accessed January 13, 2016, http:// biblehub.com/commentaries/mhcw/matthew/18.htm.

Chapter 7: A Truer Mission

1. Kieran Flanagan and Peter C. Jupp, eds., *A Sociology of Spirituality* (Hampshire, UK/Burlington, VT: Ashgate, 2007), 207.

Chapter 8: A Growing Justice

1. Scripturetext.com.
2. Brandon Hatmaker, *Barefoot Church Primer* (n.p.: Missio, 2012), week 4.
3. http://cullinanelaw.com/central-texas-nonprofit-facts/.

Chapter 9: A Fresh Perspective

1. Horace Walpole, in a letter to Lady Ossory, August 15, 1776, in *The Yale Edition of Horace Walpole's Correspondence,* vol. 32 (Yale University Press, 1937), 315.
2. Simran Khurana, "Nice Quotations," About.com, accessed January 14, 2016, http://quotations.about.com/od/cutequotes/a /NiceQuotations.htm.

ABOUT THE AUTHOR

BRANDON IS AN author, biker, TV personality, and a huge fan of the underdog. He is founder and CEO of The Legacy Collective (www.LegacyCollective.org), a giving community focused on partnering, pioneering, and funding sustainable solutions to systemic social issues around the world. Brandon is author of *Barefoot Church: Serving the Least in a Consumer Culture*. He is married to author and speaker, Jen Hatmaker.